SOCIAL WORK PRACTICE

An Ecological Approach

John T. Pardeck

Forewords by
Roland G. Meinert and John W. Murphy

AUBURN HOUSE
Westport, Connecticut • London

Library of Congress Cataloging-in-Publication Data

Pardeck, John T.
　　　Social work practice : an ecological approach / John T. Pardeck ;
　　forewords by Roland G. Meinert and John W. Murphy.
　　　　　p.　　cm.
　　Includes bibliographical references and index.
　　ISBN 0–86569–236–X (alk. paper)
　　　1. Social Service. 2. Social case work. I. Title.
　　HV40.P256　1996
　　361.3—dc20　　　95–40691

British Library Cataloguing in Publication Data is available.

Library of Congress Catalog Card Number: 95–40691
ISBN: 0–86569–236–X

First published in 1996

Auburn House, 88 Post Road West, Westport, CT 06881
An imprint of Greenwood Publishing Group, Inc.

Printed in the United States of America

The paper used in this book complies with the
Permanent Paper Standard issued by the National
Information Standards Organization (Z39.48–1984).

10　9　8　7　6　5　4　3　2　1

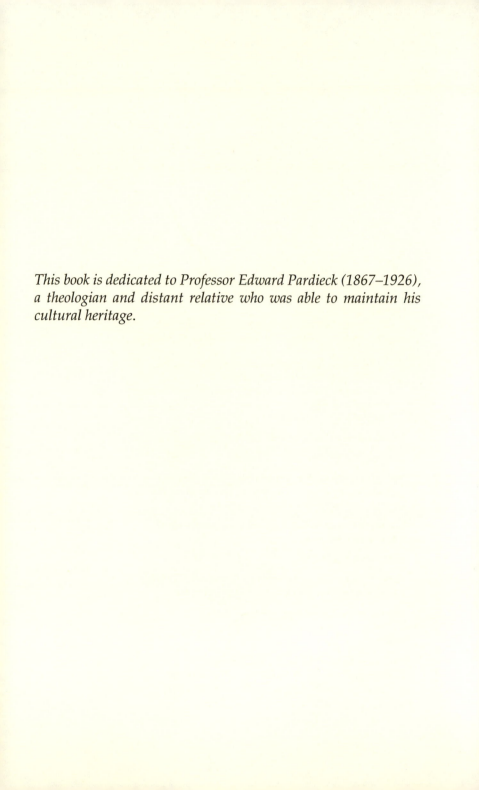

This book is dedicated to Professor Edward Pardieck (1867–1926), a theologian and distant relative who was able to maintain his cultural heritage.

Contents

Foreword

Roland G. Meinert

One of the ongoing intellectual quests in the field of social work practice as well as in social work education over the past twenty-five years has been a focused attempt to identify and arrive at a consensus about a conceptual model that captures what social work is really about. There is no one point in time that can be specifically located as the beginning of this quest. Many would point to Abraham Flexner's conclusion eighty years ago that a central deficiency about social work as a profession was that it lacked a strong, coherent, and understandable conceptual and theoretical foundation. Since that time, hundreds of social work practitioners and educators have contributed to remedying this perceived weakness, and in the last several decades this effort has accelerated. This latest work from John T. Pardeck about the ecological approach to social work practice is a significant contribution to this intellectual quest aimed at understanding one of the most misunderstood of professions. It provides a schema for how social workers should practice in the system of systems we call our social world.

The precise time that the person-in-the-environment or ecological perspective became the focal characteristic that distinguished social work from other helping professions is not exactly known. However, over the past twenty-five years numerous efforts have been made to elucidate, with all the attendant ramifications, what this means for the practice of social work. Many of these efforts have been at such an abstract level that they are meaningless to the practitioner in the field. Others have been detailed in the extreme so that their potential for generalization beyond specific situations is nonexistent. One of the specific strengths of Pardeck's work on the ecological approach to practice is its utility. The model he articulates possesses practicality and lies between useless abstractions and meaningless minutiae. He presents an ecological approach that has a goodness of fit between the various levels and variety of systems that constitute modern social work practice.

Readers should appreciate the fashion in which Pardeck understandably integrates the essential elements of the ecological approach to practice. Many authors present these separately, but the reader will find an insightful discussion and integration of how (1) the dynamic transactional process between the person and the environment, (2) the powerful and reciprocal impact of the immediate environment (behavior settings) on the person, and (3) the larger ecosystems of various ecologies all come together in a conceptually clear manner. When these are joined with a perspective resting on the scientific method and emphasizing personal and system strengths rather than the traditional focus on pathology, the model takes on a practical relevance and vitality.

This book should have a practical appeal for practitioners, whatever their adopted approach or the field in which they practice, since Pardeck illustrates the wide applicability of the model. For students of social work in both undergraduate and graduate programs, this book provides a solid exposure to the basic foundation of social work practice. Perhaps the quest for the final, definitive, and universally accepted conceptualization of social work practice will never end—nor, given the rapidly changing world in which we live, should it. However, in this quest Pardeck's well-reasoned, theoretically and scientifically grounded, and clearly written model of the ecological approach to social work practice is a valuable addition to this eight–decades-long body of work.

Foreword

John W. Murphy

Professor Pardeck's book is a textbook example of sociological imagination. According to C. Wright Mills (1959), who popularized this idea, this sort of imagination is present when the attempt is made to understand the "intersection of biography and history within society." In other words, neither psychology nor sociological determinism is appropriate, for both result in reductionism. The complexity of social life is ignored in each case, thereby resulting in simplified policies and faulty intervention.

During the past decade, however, reductionism has been an integral part of the conservative agenda. Specifically, there has been a resurgence of writing devoted to identifying psychological, physiological, and genetic sources of social problems. On the other hand, when social causes are discussed they are portrayed as structural and reified. As a result of adopting these approaches, the *processes* whereby personal initiative is blocked by the exercise of power, hierarchy, and the marginalization of individuals and groups are overlooked. But, as Mills suggests, at the nexus of these relations is where problems are created and where interventions should be directed.

What Pardeck has done is provide an ecological approach to intervention. What this means (again referring to Mills) is to move away from the idea that social issues are merely personal troubles writ large. Pardeck has demonstrated successfully, instead, that social problems are multifaceted and involve both personal and institutional variables. By making this demarche, he is trying to illustrate the need for holistic analysis. In more modern parlance, he argues that problems and their solutions are systemic in nature.

Nothing is immune to critique, according to this scenario. Persons are understood to be accountable for their actions, while institutions are indicted as contributing to social ills. For example, as Pardeck shows, improving productivity at the workplace is not simply a psychological concern. Introducing a regimen of personal incentives will be ineffective, as long as organizational impediments to growth remain intact. Interventions have to proceed, therefore, on various levels.

Pardeck maintains, and I think correctly, that this systemic style of intervention is potentially radical. In the past, microanalysis has been the preferred theory. The individual, accordingly, was blamed for all social problems. Racism, sexism, classism, and the misuse of power, for example, were not treated as institutionalized. Any discrimination that might occur was treated merely as a psychological proclivity. When viewed systematically, a personal failure (such as poor job performance) may be found to involve far more than a lack of motivation or intelligence. Institutions thought to be benign may be creating the conditions for failure.

Pardeck is not the first practitioner to call attention to this issue. Nonetheless, his new book is certainly welcome. At a time when conservatives are attempting to reassert their influence and dismiss the need for social intervention, Pardeck's orientation seems to be right on target. Systems must be changed, in short, rather than only individuals. What is radical about this notion is that entrenched sources of power are open to attack. Joblessness may not disappear unless companies are prevented from moving to Mexico. But those who wield economic power will not favor any sort of analysis that fosters such a conclusion. The beauty of systemic analysis is that arbitrary lines of societal differentiation are ignored; research is encouraged to proceed wherever the data lead.

REFERENCE

Mills, C. W. (1959). *The sociological imagination.* London: Oxford University Press.

Preface

This book provides an orientation to the role of social work practice within the human services. It differentiates the unique contributions of social work and explains how the theoretical traditions found in the field of social work support an ecological approach to practice.

The author has made an effort to define the goals, commitments, and approaches that have emerged out of the history of social work and to relate this history of the field to the concepts and values central to an ecological approach to practice. He stresses that an ecological orientation to practice is the most fruitful approach for a unifying and integrating intellectual and scientific force that may ultimately bring together the often fragmented and competing ideas emerging from the micro- and macrolevels of practice.

This book describes the operation of a variety of models of individual and group intervention. From this standpoint, the work is clearly grounded in an eclectic approach to practice. It is argued that the scope of the challenges confronting social workers can be best met by a critical but open-minded approach to the wealth of theoretical and empirical research generated not only in the field of social work but also in the related disciplines of psychology and sociology.

The reader is introduced to a variety of intervention models and the relevance of these models to the problems encountered in social work practice. The author focuses a great deal of attention on interventions, such as consultation, training, and organizational development. These levels of intervention are critical to effective social work practice grounded in an ecological perspective.

Three unifying themes are emphasized in this book. The first theme, found throughout, is the importance of practitioners viewing human growth and development as central to effective practice. The author concludes that this is a central goal that defines and distinguishes an ecological approach to social work practice from other forms of social intervention. The second theme is an affirmation of a systems approach as a core perspective for conceptualizing client problems and concerns. The ecological perspective views human beings as social organisms that transact with each other; these transactions can then inhibit or nurture individual growth and development.

The final theme emphasizes the process of transaction as the central dynamic determining the fit of the person with the environment. The traditional intrapsychic view of human behavior, grounded in the disease model, tends to de-emphasize the importance of the pressures of the social environment on the person. An ecological approach addresses individual, group, and community factors that define the social environment. From this orientation, the unique contributions of an ecological approach to social work practice emerge.

STRUCTURE OF THIS BOOK

Chapters 1 and 2 focus on an introduction to the ecological approach. Specifically, Chapter 1 emphasizes the changing nature of the human services and how an ecological perspective responds appropriately to these changes. The author introduces a model for ecological intervention and offers its philosophical underpinnings. He stresses the training and education needs for effective practice, placing special emphasis on the scientific concerns and commitments critical to effective social work practice.

Chapter 2 offers a review of general systems theory and the applications of this theory to changing communities and, ultimately, people. The author reviews theoretical and empirical differences between open and closed systems and offers implications of these differences for practice.

Chapters 3 through 6 cover the various strategies used to conduct social intervention grounded in the ecological approach. Chapter 3 reviews the traditional individual-oriented approaches to intervention and offers a critique of those interventions that can be used with an ecological approach. Chapter 4 covers the various group approaches to treatment that can be used in ecological assessment and treatment. Chapter 5 emphasizes the role of consultation and training in social work practice. Chapter 6 offers the classical theories of organizational behavior and strategies for using these theories in organizational and community development.

Chapters 7 and 8 focus on social work assessment grounded in an ecological approach. Chapter 7 reviews the importance of assessment to effective practice as well as the strengths and limitations of computer technology in ecological assessment. The author also explores the relationship of theory and research to an ecological approach to practice. Chapter 8 presents numerous clinical instruments that can be used in practice. The theoretical and scientific grounding of these clinical instruments is offered, including such traditional concerns as reliability and validity.

The final chapters, 9 and 10, present case studies of social work intervention grounded in an ecological approach. Chapter 9 offers a case study of ecological assessment and intervention with a family. Chapter 10 reviews a case study that illustrates how the ecological approach can be used as an idea orientation for empowering people. That case study relates how people with disabilities can be empowered through case advocacy and how this strategy can translate into meaningful changes in organizations that deny people with disabilities their basic human rights.

In conclusion, the ultimate goal of this book is to offer practitioners an emerging practice orientation grounded in ecological theory. It is emphasized that the ecological approach to practice is based in a holistic theoretical perspective that will help practitioners assess and treat problems of clients more effectively.

Acknowledgments

The author acknowledges a special debt of gratitude to Terry L. Brown for her assistance in editing this book. Special thanks goes to Jean A. Pardeck, Roland G. Meinert, and John W. Murphy for their support. The author also appreciates the encouragement of Ruth Pardeck, Lois Musick, and Burl Musick.

Chapter 1

An Ecological Approach to Practice

Mary Richmond (1917), an early twentieth-century pioneer in the field of social work, realized that the social environment plays a critical role in the social functioning of human beings. Even though Freud's intrapsychic theory of personality also competed with Richmond's ideas in the field's early development, throughout most of its history the profession of social work has never lost sight of the importance of the person-in-the-environment perspective when assessing and treating the problems of individuals, groups, and communities.

In the 1960s, a new interest emerged in Richmond's (1917) historic work, *Social Diagnosis.* During the 1960s, it became clear that clients need more than psychotherapeutic intervention to solve the complex problems of modern life. The research by Eysenck (1965) suggests that psychotherapeutic treatment had little relevance to oppressed people, who were in greater need of more basic services such as food and shelter. What became clear, as Richmond stressed, is that clients need social supports such as housing, health care, and jobs, as well as traditional services, such as social casework. Thus the tradition in social work of emphasizing both social treatment and social reform became the basis of the ecological approach that emerged in the profession in the 1970s.

The influential work of Germain (1973) and Hartman (1970) emphasized the importance of the ecological approach in the assessment and treatment of client problems. Even though the person-in-the-environment approach is not particularly novel as conceptualized by Germain and Hartman, their approaches do offer practical approaches for translating ecological theory into practice. An example is the concept of "goodness-of-fit" developed by Germain (1973). In her work, Germain illustrates how a misfit between the client and the environment can be corrected by focusing on points of transaction of the client with the environment—an approach that typically results in treating both the micro- and macrolevels of the client's social environment.

AN ECOLOGICAL APPROACH

An ecological approach to practice stresses that effective social work intervention occurs by working not only directly with clients but also with the familial, social, and cultural factors that affect their social functioning. The importance of the ecological approach for practice is that successful treatment must focus on multiple factors in the assessment and intervention process. The ecological perspective is also a dynamic approach because it integrates empirically based theories from various fields, including social work, psychology, sociology, and anthropology.

Germain (1973), Hartman (1976), and Siporin (1980) are among the core theorists in the field of social work that have developed the important assumptions and concepts of the ecological approach to practice. The work of these theorists offers strategies that allow the practitioner to move from a microlevel to a macrolevel of intervention that includes not only psychotherapy but also advocacy, policy, and planning activities.

Berger, Federico, and McBreen (1991) present a unique view of the complex interplay between the biological, psychological, social, economic, political, and physical forces that must be considered when using an ecological approach to practice. They conclude that the practitioner must have a holistic view of human behavior in order to understand how the environment affects a client's social functioning. These theorists conclude that an effective ecological approach to practice should include the following elements:

1. The person is seen as being influenced by multiple and interacting factors.
2. An emphasis is placed on growth and development and the attainment of goals.
3. A health orientation is stressed that focuses on the whole person, not on individual pathology.

What is particularly useful about the ecological approach is that it helps practitioners treat problems effectively at various levels, including individual, family, small group, and the larger society. When working with clients, the practitioner stresses a holistic approach that allows him or her to shift from a clinical role to a policy and planning role within the broad framework of the ecological approach. The ecological framework stresses the transactional relationship between environmental conditions and the human condition.

Six distinct professional roles have evolved within the ecological approach to practice (Pardeck, 1988a). Anderson (1981) has identified these roles as critical to effective social work practice. These core roles help the practitioner work effectively at various levels, including the individual, family, group, organization, and community. The six professional roles are as follow:

1. *Conferee:* Derived from the idea of conference, this role involves the practitioner taking direct action in helping clients do problem solving.
2. *Enabler:* This role focuses on actions taken when the practitioner structures, arranges, and changes events, interactions, and environmental factors to facilitate and enhance system functioning.
3. *Broker:* This is a traditional social work role that involves the practitioner linking the consumer with social supports and services.
4. *Mediator:* This role focuses on actions taken when the social worker's objective is to reconcile opposing or disparate points of view and bring the contestants together in united action.
5. *Advocate:* This role involves the practitioner securing services or resources when they are inadequate or nonexistent.
6. *Guardian:* This role involves taking actions that include a social control function or protecting clients who are not capable of protecting themselves.

The roles aforementioned obviously do not occur in a void; often they overlap. For example, the roles of enabler and conferee are difficult to separate. Furthermore, when the practitioner implements the broker role, he or she will probably do enabling and advocating on the behalf of the client. The complementarity among these roles is important, and they tend to cluster rather than remain distinct. As Pardeck (1988a) suggests, this approach to practice is a significant departure from the traditional methods used in social work practice—social casework, group work, and community organization. When using the aforementioned roles grounded in an ecological approach, a dynamic orientation to practice emerges that stresses the importance of environment for the person, growth and development of clients, and health versus pathology. Three important concepts help clarify the integrative nature of the ecological approach: transaction, behavioral setting, and ecosystem.

Transaction

The concept of transaction is a key process that provides insight into how the client interacts with his or her social environment. The transactional process suggests that a reciprocal relationship exists between the client and the environment. The environment contributes to the client's adjustment, and the client's behaviors create unique responses with the environment; thus both affect each other. What is critical about the transactional process is the focus of assessment and that treatment moves away from the individual toward the various systems within the client's environment (including the family and community) that comprise the client's larger social ecology. When there is harmony or a goodness-of-fit between the person and the environment, social treatment is not needed. However, when a misfit exists, the practitioner must work with the client and the larger social ecology to treat a client's presenting problem.

The transactional process means that clients should not be viewed as deviant, disturbed, or pathological but rather as part of a malfunctioning ecosystem. The transactional approach, for example, suggests that emotional disturbances are a result of a pattern of maladaptive transactions between the person and the environment. The practitioner may view this process as one of mutual influence; however, a more accurate interpretation may be sequential mutual influence, where A affects B, which in time affects A; or simultaneous mutual influence, where A and B form a whole that defines the situation (Pardeck, 1988a).

The process of transaction has been applied to a number of problem areas that confront clients. Sameroff and Zax (1978), for example, found evidence of a unique transactional process between schizophrenic parents and their children. They concluded that children of schizophrenic parents learn to adapt to the dysfunctional behaviors of their parents and in time appear to contribute to them. The process only begins after the child has developed the cognitive and linguistic skills to transact with the troubled parent. As the child learns to make an increasingly more significant contribution to the transactional process with the parent, evidence of disturbed behavior in the child begins to manifest itself across a larger number of social situations, such as the school and larger community. Sameroff and Zax found that the child who is viewed as highly disturbed is the one who, unfortunately, arouses disturbed reactions in more than one social setting.

The transactional process redefines the nature of social work practice. The practitioner should view the transactional process as learned patterns that may be understandable responses to a maladaptive social environment. Consequently, the traditional label of defining the client as emotionally disturbed is inappropriate and offers little to the practitioner for conducting effective treatment. Hobbs (1980) suggests that a more appropriate label might be the "disturbing client," which better communicates the transactional nature of the client with the environment.

Behavioral Setting

The concept of behavioral setting emerged from the work of Barker and Gump (1964) in their research on high schools. They discovered that the basic social ecology of the school setting has a dramatic impact on the various competencies of students. Depending on the school setting, students will find a niche that helps them adapt to a given school environment. If this does not occur, there is a breakdown in a student's social functioning. Even though Germain (1973) may not have been directly influenced by the work of

Barker and Gump, her suggestion that social functioning is affected by the goodness-of-fit between the person and environment is very similar to the work of Barker and Gump, which suggests that students must find an appropriate niche in a school system to function effectively. What is important about the research of Barker and Gump is that they found that the environment does not totally determine behavior—the individual also influences the environment. They noted that the same social environment provides different inputs to the same person should his or her behavior change.

The research by Barker and Gump (1964) offers to social work practice a novel approach for understanding the problems of clients. It illustrates that a client's behavior is not only shaped by the social environment, but also that behavioral changes in the client provide for different inputs from the environment. In other words, there is a transaction between the person and environment that results in the client influencing the various systems that, in turn, affect the client's behavior and social functioning.

What is particularly critical about the behavioral setting to social work practice is that the traditional approaches for defining client problems change dramatically. That is, the client is not seen as deviant or pathological but rather as a person who is transacting with a malfunctioning social environment. Rhodes and James (1978), for example, viewed emotional disturbances as a comprehensive problem of ongoing adaptation between the person and the environment, with any maladaptation being conceptualized as residing as much in the environmental activity on the person as in the person's activity on the environment. Thus problems of social functioning are viewed as stemming from an interactive, reciprocal, and dynamic set of forces operating between the person and environment (Pardeck, 1988a).

The process of transaction is a key concept that provides insight into how the behavioral setting and the person interact. The behavioral setting not only shapes the person (an orientation long accepted in social work practice), but the behavioral change in the client provides different input from the environment. In other words, the person and environment shape each other as the transactional process takes place.

From an ecological perspective, the behavioral setting offers the social work practitioner critical information when assessing the problems of clients. The behavioral setting of the client should be viewed not only in simple behavioral terms, as stressed in learning theory, but rather as inextricably interwoven relationships that include physical settings, people, time, and individual behavior (Pardeck, 1988a). The conglomeration of various behavioral settings of a client form the client's ecosystem.

The Ecosystem

The ecological approach to social work practice suggests that clients function in more than one ecology. The client's ecosystem is a conglomeration of these various ecologies. For example, a parent's ecosystem consists of the self, family, work, and the larger community. Each of the person's ecosystems has a dynamic impact on the person's social well-being.

The term *ecosystem* is not necessarily a novel concept to the field of social work. What is new and powerful about the concept of ecosystem is the position that the client cannot be juxtaposed with the environment and that the client is an inextricable part of the ecological system (Pardeck, 1989b). Simply put, the client becomes the defining element in the ecosystem, which is made up of interacting subsystems (including the family, the workplace, and the community).

Adjustment and development of clients is seen as a result of a client's transaction with the ecosystem that encompasses his or her total environment. Sameroff's (1975) work concluded that the connection between the person and the various ecosystems in the person's larger environment can be conceptualized as a "main effects" framework (bad environments cause emotional disturbance) or as a transactional framework (the transaction between a bad environment and personal characteristics of a client creates emotional disturbance). The adoption of a transactional framework advances the practitioner's understanding of the relationship between the person and his or her ecosystems. Sameroff (1975) concluded that the underlying assumption of the process of transaction is that the contact between the person and environment is a transaction in which each is altered by the other. For example, the mother or father who labels a child as difficult may come to treat the child as difficult regardless of the child's behavior. The child in due course will accept the "difficult" label as the central element to defining his or her self-image, thereby becoming the difficult child for all time.

The concept of ecosystem shifts the focus of understanding the individual's personality and behavioral functioning away from the person to the transactions that exist between the individual and the family, community, and other subsystems that form the person's ecosystem. The various ecosystems that clients transact with are critical to the assessment and treatment process.

HEALTH VERSUS INDIVIDUAL PATHOLOGY

The fashion in which one views health and pathology is critical to defining and treating the problems facing clients. The ecological approach stresses a health approach; traditional approaches to intervention, such as social casework, tend to stress pathology.

The early work of Thomas and Thomas (1928), through their concept of the "definition of the situation," illustrated that if something is defined as real, it is acted on as being just that. Such a process has great significance for understanding how presenting problems are defined and treated. For example, if a practitioner were strongly grounded in Freudian theory, he or she would define a problem such as depression differently from the way a behaviorist would define it. Both would also use different methods for intervention. In the area of mental health, the beliefs and values that shape the practitioner's worldview will greatly influence his or her definition of mental health and how emotional problems are treated (Pardeck, 1994).

There are three ways that one can perceive the problem of mental health: the disease model, illness model, and sickness model. As the practitioner grounded in the ecological approach realizes, how one defines mental health has a tremendous effect on the assessment and treatment process. For example, if the practitioner uses a disease model, mental health is viewed strictly in terms of the presence or absence of clearly identifiable psychological signs and symptoms. If one approaches the assessment of mental health from an illness model, he or she will not only assess psychological symptoms but also analyze the psychosocial aspects of presenting problems. What constitutes mental health is strongly shaped by how the term is defined and, if there is an absence of mental health, how one treats presenting problems (Pardeck, 1994).

A disease model is based on the physical aspect of a presenting problem. Disease is a biomedical concept that refers to the physiological features of nonhealth. As would be suspected, and as practitioners grounded in the ecology approach realize, a disease model for understanding mental health has numerous limitations. Unfortunately, this approach continues to be the dominant model for the delivery of mental health care in the United States (Illich, 1975). The major criticisms of the model are as follows:

1. It is grounded in the germ theory for explaining disease and lacks utility for understanding the multiple causes for assessing and treating mental illness.

2. It relies on the effectiveness of differential diagnosis when there is poor reliability among those making diagnoses for physical and mental disease.

3. It seeks a single best treatment to eradicate the cause of mental illness, whereas most illnesses have multiple causes.

4. It results in the dehumanization of mental health care because of overreliance on various technologies and overspecialization in the field of mental health.

5. It promotes authoritarian relationships between practitioners and clients in which the locus of responsibility is removed from the client.

6. It acknowledges only the biological aspects of mental health and does not address the psychosocial dimension of assessment and treatment.

7. It is a model of disease care delivery, not mental health care, and virtually ignores efforts aimed at prevention.

It becomes clear from these criticisms of the disease model that clients are at a distinct disadvantage because of the authoritarian nature of the approach and that they are seen as passive participants in the assessment and treatment process (Pardeck, 1994).

An illness approach to understanding mental health is different from the disease model (Pardeck, 1994). For example, an illness can exist whether a symptom is present or absent. If an individual defines himself or herself as emotionally troubled, even though symptoms are not present, mental illness does exist. This may well be defined as a lack of mental health. Rogers, Dubey, and Reich

(1979) concluded that subjective feelings concerning one's emotional well-being may even influence changes in the body's immune system, thus promoting the chances for physical disease to occur.

The third approach, the sickness model, is grounded in the concepts of status, roles, and social identity (Pardeck, 1994). This model is based in the field of sociology and largely views health or the lack of health as a label created by the larger society. The process of defining someone as sick can happen regardless of whether an illness or disease is present or absent. Minuchin (1974) focused on the psychosomatic aspect of sickness as defined by the family system. Parsons's (1951) work presented a highly developed model of sickness grounded in a sociological perspective. In the sickness model, the sick person

1. Is not responsible for the condition and cannot get better by an act of self-motivation
2. Is entitled to some exemptions from normal social activities based on the severity and nature of the illness
3. Does not like being ill and wants to get better
4. Must seek competent professional help to get better.

As Minuchin pointed out, much of one's ability to cope with sickness or illness is affected by one's ability to adapt to one's social environment. This position is also clearly an important part of Parsons's perspective on both physical and mental health. What this means is that a supportive social environment will result in those individuals who have been labeled as sick being better able to adapt and cope with disease and illness (Pardeck, 1994). Those social environments that are not supportive of sickness will result in poor adaptation for ill individuals.

All of the models for defining mental and physical health have limitations. However, the disease model appears to offer little for those concerned with the effects of the various ecosystems that affect a client's social functioning. Thus, the component that is clearly lacking in the disease model is the social and subjective nature of health. Both of these critical aspects of mental health and one's social well-being are dealt with far more effectively in the illness and sickness models. Antonovsky (1979) offered helpful insight into how mental health is understood when considering the psychosocial aspects of sickness and illness.

Antonovsky (1979) argued that mental health cannot be understood using a pathological orientation or disease model. He suggested that, instead, one should use a "Dis-ease–Ease" continuum. Antonovsky found that nearly one half of the population will suffer from some form of physical or mental illness. Some of these conditions will be disabling. Given the nature of illness and disease and the large numbers of people that are affected, it is limiting to view sickness or health from a disease perspective because it places health and disease dichotomously. Health is instead, according to Antonovsky, a highly relative issue influenced by genetics as well as one's social environment. Furthermore, mental health is largely defined by social and cultural factors (Pardeck, 1994).

Interesting enough, Antonovsky also suggests that health cannot be viewed solely as a dependent variable. Health as an independent variable may directly affect one's total life experiences, including physical disease. Health, for example, may be the prime reason determining if a person is susceptible to bacterial pathogens that are present in all individuals. In this sense, health and disease form a transaction in which each influences the other. Antonovsky (1979) concluded that his "Dis-ease–Ease" continuum allows one to assess health (or dis-ease) in a global fashion that includes the following:

1. Pain level present, from none to severe
2. The degree of functional limitation, ranging from none to severe
3. The implications of the prognosis, ranging from minor to life threatening
4. The actions that must be taken for treatment, ranging from none to immediate.

Through using these assessment criteria, Antonovsky concluded that 384 possible profiles can be developed to identify one's level of physical and mental health. This is far from the dichotomous perspective of health versus disease endorsed by the disease model (Pardeck, 1994).

An ecological approach to practice views social functioning and one's total well-being from a health perspective that includes the psychological and social aspects of illness and sickness. Such a view, as suggested by Antonovsky (1979), offers a more holistic view of emotional health and total well-being that reinforces the active participation of the client in the assessment and treatment process.

SCIENTIFIC PRACTICE

The ecological approach is grounded in scientific practice. The ecological perspective, like scientific practice, is built on knowledge generated through scientific inquiry. The ecological approach, like scientific practice, emphasizes an objective approach to gathering data when assessing problems confronting clients. Like a scientist, the practitioner using an ecological orientation searches for causes to problems and is systematic in his or her approach to assessment and treatment of presenting problems. Monette, Sullivan, and De-Jong (1990) offered the following steps that will prove useful to practitioners using an ecological framework in assessing and treating problems.

Problem Assessment

During this initial stage, the practitioner must decide which ecosystems are involved in a problem—individual, group, community, or societal—and whether effective intervention is possible.

Formulation of Intervention Strategy

The practitioner must develop a strategy for intervention that will be effective in alleviating a presenting problem. The intervention is based on a holistic understanding of the client that lends itself to a variety of techniques for change, including crisis intervention, vocational training, and behavior modification.

Implementation

The practitioner proceeds to the point of implementing the intervention strategy as outlined in the preceding stages. He or she must collect data as a part of the implementation stage to assess the effectiveness of the intervention strategy in changing the client or the ecosystems in which the client transacts.

Evaluation

The practitioner must evaluate the effectiveness of the intervention strategy implemented. Questions such as these should be asked concerning the success of intervention: Were the treatment goals achieved? What were the costs of the intervention? Were there any unintended consequences brought about by the intervention? Which components of the intervention process seemed to be most effective in producing the change that resulted?

Closure

The final stage of the intervention process is drawing conclusions about the social treatment efforts of the practitioner. The extent to which the intervention has been effective must be determined as well as the degree to which the goals of the intervention were not achieved. The practitioner might suggest to the client at this stage other sources that might help the client cope with problems that still need to be resolved. During closure, the practitioner looks back over what has been accomplished and forward to directions and alternatives for the future.

Reid (1978) suggested a number of changes that can help the practitioner in the human service delivery system and enhance the aforementioned stages of scientific practice:

1. Build research questions into the daily routine of collecting case information rather than simply attempting to devise problems from the data.
2. Devote special care to the selection and development of recording formats. Many data in agency records are ambiguous and haphazard, and the practitioner must organize these data in a rational format.
3. Structure practice in such a fashion that goals and targets are empirically based and the intervention is clearly specified. This helps the practitioner use case records more effectively when implementing social intervention.
4. Rely on multiple data sources. In addition to using the impressions of the practitioner, other empirically based methods (such as clinical

instruments and focused direct observation) should supplement the practitioner's impressions of the client.

Using a scientific approach is critical to effective practice grounded in the ecological approach. Not only will social work practice improve through the scientific approach, but the practitioner will increase his or her understanding of the various ecosystems—the family, school, and community—that influence the social environment of clients.

EMPIRICAL KNOWLEDGE VERSUS PERSONAL KNOWLEDGE

Practitioners using the ecological approach to practice use both empirical and personal knowledge as sources for implementing scientific practice. Empirical knowledge is grounded in traditional scientific inquiry, whereas personal knowledge is based on one's objective interpretation of personal experiences.

An empirical approach typically uses data as the source for knowledge development. Facts are developed when data are collected on a continuing basis and repeatedly yield the same results. This approach is also referred to as positivism. Even though personal knowledge often lacks the focused rigor demanded by an empirical approach to practice, Berger, Federico, and McBreen (1991, p. 10) suggested that personal knowledge is the basis of all objective knowledge. In fact, it might be superior to empirical knowledge because it depends on experience—sensory experience—instead of data gained in other ways. Personal knowledge is nevertheless critical to effective practice. It is, however, different because it is not always measurable in the same fashion as empirically based knowledge.

Practitioners using the ecological framework for social treatment will utilize both empirical and personal knowledge in the assessment and treatment of client problems. The practitioner uses empirical knowledge when he or she has the client complete a scale measuring some aspect of social functioning. Other empirical knowledge includes gathering information on the client's age, income, and educational background. Personal knowledge is critical to effective ecological practice because it is based on experience.

In a certain sense, personal knowledge deals with the more abstract aspects of the human experience involving the body, mind, and soul. These highly abstract aspects of the human experience should be seen as complementing the empirically based knowledge used in the assessment and treatment process.

AN ECOLOGICAL STRATEGY FOR SOCIAL INTERVENTION

As noted by Hobbs (1980), two major prerequisites must be accomplished prior to the implementation of an ecological approach to practice. First, the practitioner must identify sources of discord in the client's ecosystem as well as sources of strengths that can be used to improve the goodness-of-fit between the person and the environment. Second, once assessment has been conducted focusing on the client's goodness-of-fit with his or her environment, the practitioner must develop a treatment plan that improves the transactional process between client and environment. In contrast to traditional approaches to intervention, which are often narrow and view the individual client as the primary focus of assessment and treatment, an ecological approach offers a more holistic approach to assessment and intervention (Pardeck, 1988b).

The following social intervention model presents specific steps that help translate ecological assessment into treatment. The model is a translation of community psychologist Plas's (1981) approach to the field of social work. This treatment model does not differ a great deal from traditional approaches to practice, which stress the importance of data gathering for assessment that leads to intervention. However, what is significantly different about the following approach is that each step of assessment and social intervention stresses the importance of micro- and macrolevel systems in treating client problems, and that the transactional process between persons and their environments is the focus of ecological treatment. The following model is the focus of ecological treatment:

1. Entering the system
2. Mapping the ecology
3. Assessing the ecology
4. Creating a vision of change
5. Coordinating and communicating

6. Reassessing
7. Evaluating.

Entering the System

Once a decision has been made to offer social work services to a client, the first step in intervention is to enter the client's ecosystem. This process is accomplished by (1) assessing all critical relationships in the client's life and (2) identifying a point of entry into the client's world. When assessing the relationships of the client, the practitioner must focus on the various subsystems that the client transacts with. The practitioner gains important information from these systems that will shape the social intervention process. The practitioner must also identify a point at which he or she can enter the client's world. This might be accomplished through interviews that involve not only the client but also those within the client's family and other critical subsystems. By involving individuals from various subsystems in the client's world, the practitioner can begin to identify sources of discord as well as strength in the client's ecosystem (Pardeck, 1988b).

Mapping the Ecology

The practitioner begins the process of mapping the ecology once he or she has entered the client's world. At this stage, systems theory is used to analyze the client's social environment. The social worker analyzes the various subsystems of the client's social environment to identify the individuals and events that are pertinent to the problems confronting the client.

Subsystems can be placed in two broad categories: people and events. Events included are those considered to be typical occasions within the client's world that enhance both positive and negative feelings and behaviors. These events are identified through interaction of representatives of various subsystems that form the client's ecosystem. These events include the content of the interaction between the client and his or her family as well as the client's interaction with others in the community. The information obtained through monitoring events in the client's social environment is critical to the mapping process (Pardeck, 1988b).

Identifying critical people and events in the client's social environment can be accomplished through a number of approaches, including structured interviews with the client and significant individuals in the client's ecosystem. Numerous clinical instruments have been created that help practitioners assess accurately a client's presenting problem. These instruments are the focus of Chapter 8. The sociogram can also be a valuable tool for mapping the social ecology of clients. Hartman's (1976) family sculpturing technique can be a useful tool for mapping family-based problems.

Assessing the Ecology

Once the practitioner has mapped the ecology, the information gathered must be interpreted. During the assessment stage, the practitioner is searching for primary problems and the major areas of strength in the client's ecosystem. A critical aspect of this stage is to describe the relationships and reoccurring themes in the client's life.

Reoccurring events in the client's ecosystem need to be noted. For example, are the same individuals always present at those events that appear to be critical to understanding the client's presenting problem? Which events in the client's social environment are seen as important by significant others in the client's world? This information allows the social worker to assign weights to those relationships that appear to be most important. Those persons and events that are mentioned most often are considered to carry the greatest influence with respect to maintaining the ecosystem of the client as well as creating change (Pardeck, 1988b).

The social worker's assessment strategy when analyzing the client's ecosystem is designed to elicit information concerning those people and situations that support positive behaviors and those that support negative feelings and actions. Once the social worker has assessed strengths, weaknesses, and influential relationships, he or she can interpret these data for the client and significant others in the client's ecosystem. The most central stage of the intervention process is next (Pardeck, 1988b).

Creating the Vision of Change

Once the practitioner reaches this stage in the intervention process, the benefits of assessment and mapping the ecology begin to
be realized. This stage of the intervention process includes all of
those individuals in the client's ecosystem can effect impact
change. Through this process, the practitioner stresses the areas
that need to be changed to improve the client's social functioning.

As the practitioner focuses on the changes needed, it is critical
that he or she emphasize the entire ecosystem of the client and build
on the strengths present in this ecology. When significant individuals and, in particular, the client have agreed to the intervention
method, the next stage is to implement the plan of action.

Coordinating and Communicating

An important role of the social worker during the intervention
process is to coordinate and communicate with those in the client's
ecosystem. Much of the change effort is in the hands of those
significant persons in the client's ecosystem. Simply put, the social
worker offers support and facilitates the continuing change efforts,
such as telephone calls, home visits, and other supportive efforts.
Given the fact that the client's ecosystem is dynamic and not static,
the practitioner must be open to the possibility that the intervention
efforts may have to be modified and reevaluated. This is the focus
of the next stage.

Reassessing

The change efforts that have been agreed to by the client and
significant others in the ecosystem may have to be reassessed if
treatment is less than successful. The exploration of this possibility
is largely accomplished through the traditional assessment method
of interviewing the client and others in the client's ecosystem. If the
intervention efforts are seen as successful, the practitioner can
move toward termination with the client and other significant
individuals in the client's ecosystem.

Evaluating

The reassessment phase is focused on outcomes; the final stage, evaluation, is concerned with the total evaluation of the treatment process. The social worker can gather information through informal meetings with the client and others relevant to the treatment process, or this evaluation can be done through a structured questionnaire. The total evaluation of the intervention process has a useful purpose in that it helps the practitioner improve the ecosystem–oriented assessment-intervention treatment for future cases.

HUMAN SERVICES AND THE ECOLOGICAL APPROACH

A number of writers (e.g., Vega & Murphy, 1990) have suggested that the current organization of the human services field does not serve clients well. The following is a series of questions that summarize the dissatisfaction with the human services field. Using an ecological approach to human services delivery will correct many of these deficiencies.

Is the Medical Model a Sufficiently Comprehensive and Useful Approach for Organizing Human Services?

The medical model is based on a disease approach for explaining problems facing clients and is heavily grounded in a philosophical premise of the separation of mind and body. Out of this questionable dichotomy, a notion has emerged that problems in social functioning are caused by individual pathology. This view is obviously contrary to the ecological approach to practice, which stresses a holistic orientation for assessing and treating problems of clients. When practitioners are grounded in an ecological orientation to practice, they firmly reject the notion of separate and isolatable psychological and physical states within the person (Blocher & Biggs, 1983).

In traditional social work practice, which tends to emphasize individual pathology, the absence of specific symptoms or identifiable pathology suggests that the person is functioning at a reasonable level of well-being. The individual is commonly viewed as emotionally healthy when he or she is not experiencing bothersome or significant symptoms. Consequently, a client's well-being is based on identifying known symptoms, causes, and treatments.

The shortcoming of the medical model is that effects of various social and cultural factors influencing one's total well-being are not considered. An ecological approach to human services delivery calls for banishing the disease model to practice and suggests that such a simplistic approach is intellectually bankrupt (Blocher & Biggs, 1983).

Who Is the Client for Human Services Delivery?

An ecological approach to practice suggests that the ultimate client system of concern is society itself. The social practitioner grounded in the ecological perspective is well aware of the impact of social forces on the well-being of clients. He or she realizes that the problems facing many people in society are a result of poor organization and management of human affairs (Blocher & Biggs, 1983).

Much of the human services delivery system is built on a philosophy that blames the victim as the cause of social problems. The person-blame philosophy diverts attention from the real issues and results in a human services delivery system that is largely counterproductive to client well-being (Blocher & Biggs, 1983). As suggested by Szasz (1961) and Halleck (1971), many problems confronting people are not personal failure but are more accurately defined as societed failure. It can be argued that the real solutions to numerous problems facing people may well be political in nature, because the clients of human services are often powerless or otherwise disadvantaged in society. An ecological approach to practice suggests that practitioners have an obligation to pursue political changes that improve the human services delivery system. Karger and Stoesz (1990, p. 340) have defined this kind of intervention as "political social work practice."

When organizing human services around a person-blame philosophy, the larger social context of the causes of human problems is simply overlooked. This view perpetuates a series of primitive and partial remedies that enhance remedies that merely increase suffering and injustice. Recent work by Vega and Murphy (1990) has pointed to the importance of a massive reconceptualization of the human services delivery system, which calls for changing the social structures that ultimately promote social problems.

What Are the Goals of the Human Services Delivery System?

These goals change dramatically when moving toward an ecological approach to practice. If service delivery is based on an individual pathology model, the emphasis is on intrapsychic theories and models for dealing with problems of clients. If the social practitioner assesses and treats the problems of clients from an ecological orientation, the goals of human service delivery are not only to change clients but also to change the ecosystems that inhibit client functioning (Blocher & Biggs, 1983).

One of the major goals of social work practice based on the ecological approach is to change the human services worker's orientation to the definition and treatment of client problems. If practitioners view client problems from an individual pathology approach, it is unlikely that they will be effective in their service delivery activities. However, if practitioners assess and treat problems as a result of dysfunctional transactions of clients with their social environments, the goals of human services delivery move to a more holistic approach. When using an ecological approach to practice, such features of the client's environment—including diseasism, racism, sexism, unemployment, or restricted educational opportunity—are critical to social intervention. The empirical research concluding that mental health problems are more likely to be found among the lower socioeconomic classes is well known to practitioners grounded in an ecological perspective (Dohrenwend & Dohrenwend, 1969). It is also not unexpected to find more problems in social functioning among those who are experiencing disorganization and insecure social environments (Bradshaw, 1969).

The work of Bronfenbrenner (1979), an ecological theorist, provided insight into human development that must be built into the goals of human services delivery. This view conceptualizes human development as the product of a lifelong process of engagement between the individual and the environment. Behavior can only be understood fully when viewing the person as part of a larger ecosystem. From this perspective, disorders or dysfunctions that are barriers to development are best viewed and most effectively prevented or remediated within the natural environment in which they occur. This perspective is extremely critical to the way practitioners design treatment intervention (Blocher & Biggs, 1983).

An ecological approach changes the goals of human services delivery. This is largely a result of the theoretical grounding of the ecological approach. One of the important propositions of ecological theory is that intrapsychic treatments have little relevance to solving problems of clients. Another is that the larger society is viewed as a system that can remediate problems facing clients. When there is a goodness-of-fit between society and individuals, personal growth and development can occur. When there is a misfit, individuals will experience problems, including depression, medical ailments, anxiety, and substance abuse. Thus the core goals of the human services delivery system should be to create a nurturing environment aimed at preventing social problems and to improve the goodness-of-fit between the client and society when breakdown has occurred.

CONCLUSION

The ecological perspective defines human problems as outcomes of transaction between the environment and individuals. Conceptualizing presenting problems of clients in this fashion moves social work practice back to the early work of Mary Richmond. Richmond was well aware that a disjunction between the person and the environment could have negative consequences on an individual's physical, emotional, and social well-being. Germain (1973) and Hartman (1976) concluded that this focus is the distinguishing and unifying theme of modern-day social work practice.

Present-day ecological theory defines the problems of clients in an enlightened fashion and thus demands that problems of clients must be defined in new ways. Ultimately, the goals of the human services delivery system must change. The emphasis of human services must be to create a better fit between the person and the environment. Such thinking separates social work from the more traditional disciplines of psychology and psychiatry, which have a tendency to stress individual pathology models for diagnosis and intervention. Moreover, an ecological approach suggests that the traditional methods of social casework, group work, and community practice are dated. These methods are largely built on traditional approaches that define the individual as the major cause of social problems.

The ecological approach provides practitioners with an integrative approach to practice. It offers new and innovative strategies for assessment and treatment of client problems. Practitioners grounded in the ecological approach view the person as influenced by multiple and interacting factors. Persons are also seen as influencing the ecosystems that shape their behavioral settings. The ecological approach stresses growth and development and the attainment of goals. Finally, it is an orientation that focuses on the whole person and his or her environment, not on individual pathology. An ecological approach to practice means that social workers work not only with clients but also with the ecosystems that affect a client's social functioning.

REFERENCES

Anderson, J. (1981). *Social work methods and processes.* Belmont, CA: Wadsworth.

Antonovsky, A. (1979). *Health, stress, and coping.* San Francisco, CA: Jossey-Bass.

Barker, R., & Gump, P. (1964). *Big school, small school.* Stanford, CA: Stanford University Press.

Berger, R. L., Federico, R. C., & McBreen, J. T. (1991). *Human behavior: A perspective for the helping professions* (3rd ed.). New York: Longman.

Blocher, D. H., & Biggs, D. A. (1983). *Counseling psychology in community settings.* New York: Springer.

Bradshaw, C. E. (1969). The poverty culture. *Childhood Education, 46,* 79–84.

Bronfenbrenner, U. (1979). *The ecology of human development.* Cambridge, MA: Harvard University Press.

Dohrenwend, B. P., & Dohrenwend, B. S. (1969). *Social status and psychological disorder.* New York: Wiley.

Eysenck, H. J. (1965). The effects of psychotherapy. *International Journal of Psychiatry, 1,* 97–144.

Germain, C. (1973). An ecological perspective in casework. *Social Casework, 54,* 323–330.

Halleck, S. L. (1971). *Politics of therapy*. New York: Science House.

Hartman, A. (1970). To think about the unthinkable. *Social Casework, 50,* 467–474.

––––––. (1976). *Finding families: An ecological approach to family assessment in adoption*. Beverly Hills, CA: Sage.

Hobbs, N. (1980). An ecologically oriented, service-based system for the classification of handicapped children. In S. Salzinger, J. Antrobus, & J. Glick (Eds.), *The ecosystem of the "sick" child: Implications for classification and intervention for disturbed and mentally retarded children* (pp. 272–290). New York: Academic Press.

Illich, I. (1975). *Medical nemesis: The expropriation of health*. London: Calder & Boyars.

Karger, H., & Stoesz, D. (1990). *American social welfare policy: A structural approach*. New York: Longman.

Minuchin, S. (1974). *Families and family therapy*. Cambridge, MA: Harvard University Press.

Monette, R. R., Sullivan, T. J., & DeJong, C. R. (1990). *Applied social research: Tool for the human services* (2nd ed.). Chicago: Holt, Rinehart and Winston.

Pardeck, J. T. (1988a). An ecological approach for social work practice. *Journal of Sociology and Social Welfare, 15,* 133–142.

––––––. (1988b). Social treatment through an ecological approach. *Clinical Social Work Journal, 16,* 92–104.

––––––. (1994). *Using bibliotherapy in clinical practice: A guide to self-help books*. Westport, CT: Greenwood Press.

Parsons, T. (1951). *The social system*. New York: The Free Press.

Plas, J. (1981). The psychologist in the school community: A liaison role. *School Psychology Review, 10,* 72–81.

Reid, W. (1978). The social agency as a research machine. *Journal of Social Service Research, 7,* 11–23.

Rhodes, W., & James, P. (1978). *Emotionally disturbed and deviant children*. Englewood Cliffs, NJ: Prentice-Hall.

Richmond, M. (1917). *Social diagnosis*. New York: Russell Sage Foundation.

Rogers, M. P., Dubey, D., & Reich, P. (1979). The influence of the psyche and the brain on immunity and disease susceptibility. *Psychosomatic Medicine, 41,* 147–164.

Sameroff, A. (1975). Transactional models in early social relations. *Human Development, 18,* 65–79.

Sameroff, A., & Zax, A. (1978). A search of schizophrenia: Young offspring of schizophrenic women. In L. Wynne (Ed.), *The nature of schizophrenic women* (pp. 430–441). New York: Wiley.

Siporin, M. (1980). Ecological systems theory in social work. *Journal of Sociology and Social Welfare, 7,* 507–532.

Szasz, T. S. (1961). *The myth of mental illness.* New York: Haber.

Thomas, W. I., & Thomas, E. S. (1928). *The child in America.* New York: Knopf.

Vega, W. A., & Murphy, J. W. (1990). *Culture and the restructuring of community mental health.* Westport, CT: Greenwood Press.

Chapter 2

The Community as Client

The community is one of the most important client systems that practitioners work with on a daily basis. An ecological approach to practice views the community as a critical system that must be included in the assessment and treatment process. Individual problems cannot be assessed or treated appropriately unless these problems are understood in the context of the community system. Social workers can view the impact of the community on individual functioning through systems analysis. A systems orientation includes organizational development and restructuring, creation of settings, and evaluation as critical strategies for changing communities.

Social workers grounded in an ecological approach intervene in a wide variety of social systems when working with communities. An important intervention strategy is to help individuals think about and act in a meaningful fashion in the various social systems that comprise the community. All social systems (including the family, school, and other small systems) are part of what we refer to as the larger community. Changing the smaller systems that comprise the community will ultimately change the community (Blocher & Biggs, 1983).

When working with the social systems that comprise the community, practitioners must focus on how individuals behave in interaction with each other. Social work intervention at the community level is dealing with processes that differ only in complexity from those at the individual level. The core systems that practitioners work with when doing community intervention are groups and organizations.

SYSTEMS THEORY

A system can be viewed as a whole comprised of individual parts. When change occurs in one part, the other parts of the system are affected. For example, when a practitioner is able to implement a latchkey program in a community, this change will have an effect on other systems in the community, including the family and workplace. Systems theory focuses on linkages and relationships that connect individuals with each other and with the larger environment.

Berger, Federico, and McBreen (1991) suggest that a system is a series of smaller units nestled inside progressively larger ones. Planet Earth is affected by a city that discharges untreated sewage into a river, because this waste will ultimately affect a river. These smaller systems, the city and river, contribute to the total ecology of the Earth. Similar relationships are present for various human systems—individuals, families, complex organizations, societies, and whole cultures—and ultimately the entire human community. Each system affects the others.

Berger and associates (1991) stress that practitioners must realize that larger systems, such as communities, are composed of smaller systems, such as small groups and families. Systems theory provides a paradigm that focuses on multiple levels of phenomena simultaneously and emphasizes the interaction between behavioral units. The result is that a systems view helps social workers understand behavior in context and illustrates how these units comprise the larger ecology of the human community.

OPEN AND CLOSED SYSTEMS

At a conceptual level, systems can be viewed as open or closed. Whereas open systems are generally healthy, closed systems are typically dysfunctional. Open systems are those that exchange matter and energy with their environments. For example, a candle covered with a glass jar is similar to a closed system because it lacks oxygen and gradually goes out. When the glass jar is removed, the lighted candle exchanges oxygen and carbon dioxide with the atmosphere; then it is like an open system (Blocher & Biggs, 1983).

Systems theory suggests that all systems attempt to maintain a steady state as they transact with their environments. Furthermore, they are self-regulating. There is a tendency to return to an original state even after the larger ecology changes. Obviously, this can result in a functional or dysfunctional system. An example would be a family in a community that is in transition. If the transition is toward crime and poverty, this change will ultimately affect that family. If the family is a functional system, it will attempt to maintain this steady state regardless of the larger dysfunctional community. Social work intervention is critical for such a family when a community experiences general social disorganization.

The exchange process occurring between systems and the larger social environment are referred to as input and output. The resources used by the system to obtain goals are called input. Likewise, output refers to the products created by systems after inputs have been processed.

Through the input/output process, the practitioner can begin to realize the delicate balance between the family system and the larger community. The larger community must provide families with quality schools as well as economic and social supports in order for families to operate at an optimal level. If this kind of input is not forthcoming from the community, families will not contribute positive output in exchange. What emerges is a family system that gradually becomes a closed system characterized by abuse, neglect, and other kinds of dysfunctional behaviors. Thus the practitioner can see clearly that healthy families often thrive in healthy communities. Disorganized communities create an environment that can well influence families in a negative fashion (Blocher & Biggs, 1983).

Open systems tend to display equifinality; that is, similar results can be obtained from different kinds of beginning conditions. For example, two infants, one born prematurely and the other born at full term, will look very different at birth. However, if both are provided appropriate care and nutrition, the differences will disappear as they move through the life cycle. Even though the children's initial state was very different, human beings typically attain similar states of physical growth and development if properly nourished.

The key to effective social work practice grounded in an ecological orientation is to provide the systems that comprise the larger environment with the nutriments to achieve optimal development. When this input is not present, systems tend to move toward a closed state. The practitioner's role is to alter or prevent this kind of negative transaction between a system and its larger environment.

SYSTEMS THEORY AND PRACTICE

Systems theory allows the practitioner to examine complex social patterns, structures, processes, and ultimately problems within a community. From a community perspective, a change in one part of a community has consequences for other parts of a community. Practice at the community level is designed to influence change in a subsystem of a community with the intent of increasing the total functioning of the larger community system.

Systems theory is an excellent strategy for understanding the interrelationships and interconnectedness among different aspects of a phenomenon. It is this orientation that makes systems theory an intricate part of the ecological approach and a powerful tool for understanding and changing communities.

Practitioners realize that a community is made up of interdependent parts. The idea of community reflects shared agreement on what people feel is important. This agreement may be based on geography, customs, mores, values, beliefs, and norms. Such agreement results in the interdependence of community members. Obviously, communities vary in size and complexity; the larger and more complex a community system is, the greater the practitioner's challenges are in the assessment and intervention process. The social worker realizes the complexity and interrelatedness of a community when it is affected by natural disasters, strikes, and riots. When these kinds of issues arise, the interdependence of a community is altered dramatically (Blocher & Biggs, 1983).

Systems theory provides the social worker with a perspective that suggests the tremendous complexity and interdependence of human beings in a modern society. Through dynamic assessment of a community, the social worker can identify key variables, causes, and transactions that help explain overall community functioning. This kind of information can lead to effective social change.

COMMUNITY INTERVENTION

Effective ecological social work practice views the community as a client system that must be considered critical to social intervention regardless of the level of intervention. For example, family treatment cannot be effective unless the practitioner includes the community and its various subsystems in the total treatment process of the family.

A community is a system in which, through collective efforts of its individual parts composed of people, goals can be achieved. People who are part of a community must have their basic needs and expectations met if communities are to flourish. An ecological perspective suggests that patterns and forms of groups (including the family, organizations, and communities) are what contribute to individual behavior. However, individuals are not passive recipients of this input from the larger social ecology. Through transaction, individuals are shaped by their environments, and they in turn affect their environments. This means that individual social functioning can never be understood fully unless the practitioner includes the impact of the environment on the person. Furthermore, the environment must always be viewed as a series of subsystems made up of individuals interacting with each other. There is mutuality between individuals and ultimately between the systems that make up the larger community (Blocher & Biggs, 1983).

Most communities are resistant to change because a great deal of energy is directed at maintenance. Systems are generally difficult to change. Consequently, planning efforts by social practitioners will be painfully difficult because of community members' heavy emphasis on maintaining the community as it exists. A strategy that social workers who are attempting to change a community can use is to involve the community in its own self-examination or evaluation. Too often within a community, there is a perception that only one way is acceptable for conducting community activities. This kind of consensus inhibits rational planning; consequently, many social problems often go unanswered because the community directs most of its energy at maintaining the status quo.

CHANGING COMMUNITIES

Even though communities are conservative social systems that have a tendency to direct most activities at maintenance of the status quo, social workers use a number of change strategies. These include democratic participation, collaborative activities, and task-oriented social change (Blocher & Biggs, 1983).

Democratic Participation

One of the most effective ways to provide people with a feeling of ownership in change activities is through democratic participation. By allowing community members input through the democratic process, change is likely to occur. When social workers are involved in community planning activities, these activities should enrich community members and better prepare them for meeting future community needs. The goal of practice at the community level should be to create the "competent community" (Isoce, 1974, p. 608).

When community members become involved in community change through the democratic process, people learn that they can control their own lives and ultimately improve the quality of their neighborhoods. These activities help create positive attitudes about the self and other community members. Social workers must realize that efforts to change communities will only be successful if they are grounded in democratic values.

Successful community planning should trigger the development of new community leadership. People should learn how to help themselves. They should be taught to take responsibility for the self and, in general, make a greater contribution to the larger community. These kinds of results will occur only if community members feel that they have genuine input into change activities through the democratic process (Blocher & Biggs, 1983).

Collaborative Activities

Collaborative activities are based on discussion and interaction among those who will be affected by social change. In a certain sense, collaborative activities make the democratic process work. A goal of the social worker involved in community change efforts should be to involve individuals and groups with similar interests in the collaborative process. The consensus that emerges from this kind of collaboration should be the guiding principle for shaping community change efforts. Change efforts are almost never successful if imposed from above or through top-down efforts. This kind of process often means that those who are most affected by change will resist it because they have not given it sanction through the democratic process. Conflict is sure to emerge from a top-down approach to community change because it does not take into account the needs and interests of community members often most affected by the change. Social practitioners working with a community system must help those attempting to change it from above realize that they must work in collaboration with community members if there is to be a successful outcome (Blocher & Biggs, 1983).

Social workers have the skills, knowledge, and expertise to facilitate collaboration among those who wish to bring about change. Their knowledge of social behavior prepares them well for working effectively with individuals and groups involved in collaborative efforts. Thus social work training and education informs them that they must communicate genuine respect to community members, and that humility is important to successful community change efforts.

Task-Oriented Social Change

Another basic principle of the democratic approach to social change is the task-oriented approach. This process of planned social change at the community level is focused on the nature of the problem to be solved and the human needs to be met. Given that vested interest groups often wish to maintain the status quo within the community, a task-oriented social change effort may be perceived as threatening. Practitioners must be sure that they are not manipulated by these powerful vested interest groups.

When using the task-oriented approach, the social worker should follow a number of steps (Zastrow, 1992, p. 511):

1. Identify potential problems by helping community members describe them.
2. Help community members reach a tentative agreement on the problems that need to be solved.
3. Challenge nonresolvable problems.
4. Raise additional problems that may be created when priorities are reached and strategies for change are agreed on.
5. Seek the involvement of other community members who have not been involved in the process up to this point.
6. Decide on the strategy that will be used to solve identified problems.

These steps demand that the task-oriented change process be democratic. It is a process grounded on the position that social planning is a bottom-up approach. Community members who become involved in task-oriented social change efforts will probably develop strong emotional identification with the change process. This identification can be an effective tool for motivating powerful community groups to work for the adoption of proposals to improve the community. The social work practitioner plays a critical role in ensuring that the planned change effort is not compromised when the powerful members within the community structure endorse the plan. Modification of the planned social change effort may be necessary to win the endorsement of powerful vested interest groups, but these modifications may make the initially agreed-on plan ineffective (Blocher & Biggs, 1983).

RESISTANCE TO SOCIAL CHANGE

Planning social change at the macrolevel in many respects is no different than at the microlevel. When doing intervention at either level, democratic principles are always involved. The social worker avoids imposing arbitrary values on the larger community; likewise, the practitioner uses the same philosophy when working with clients on the individual level. Just as the individual in counseling does, the community as a client system will resist change. The practitioner grounded in the ecological perspective realizes that these kinds of phenomena are typical of systems in general, including individual clients (Blocher & Biggs, 1983).

When practitioners work with communities, the resistance to social change should be viewed as more or less typical behavior that is expected when one is involved in social intervention efforts. When doing community practice, the social worker is attempting to provide the community with new skills and resources for problem solving. This creates disequilibrium within the community. Like other systems, the community must adjust to this tension; thus the members who comprise the community feel uncomfortable. This kind of self-renewal at the macrolevel is resistance because the community as a client system aims most of its energy at maintenance.

One of the clear issues that emerges for practitioners doing community work is that they may become easily discouraged. The planned rational change that the practitioner is advocating for in the community will almost always be resisted. Practitioners must not be deterred by the intensity of the resistance. Humor is an important psychological tool that will help not only the practitioner but also community members deal with resistance (Blocher & Biggs, 1983).

As Watson (1967) pointed out, human behavior is naturally resistant to change. The practitioner must also realize that individuals are the building blocks of the community. Individuals seek stability, communities seek stability, and stability is built on habit and continuity in one's everyday life. Community social change efforts challenge the status quo, and resistance to change efforts is consequently predictable. The practitioner grounded in the ecological approach has the knowledge and skills to deal with resistance in individual clients as well as in larger social systems such as communities (Blocher & Biggs, 1983). Doing social change at both the micro- and macrolevels is the essence of ecological social work practice.

THE RESPONSIVE COMMUNITY

Social workers using the ecological approach to practice must realize that responsive communities have unique characteristics that produce ecosystems that nurture individual self-actualization. The following conditions, adopted from the work of Blocher and Biggs (1983), create a responsive community.

Vision

The responsive community provides opportunities for community members to create new visions for overcoming obstacles that have stifled development in the past. The environment must offer novelty, complexity, ambiguity, and emotional intensity that stimulate persons to action. When high levels of stimulation from the environment occur, some individuals will withdraw, but others will respond in a positive fashion. Static communities do not offer the environmental stimulants to change; thus the role of the social worker is to create in community members visions of change that move people to action. Extremely restrictive subsystems in the community (e.g., static school systems) do not offer the stimulation for change. The practitioner must work with subsystems such as schools because they are key change agents for developing responsive communities. Special programs for children, such as Head Start, can also be used as effective change agents. The critical strategy for the practitioner is to help create visions of change in critical subsystems that will eventually affect the entire community.

Participation

As stressed earlier in this chapter, meaningful participation by community members in change efforts is critical to the growth and development of community members. Community change means allowing participants to take responsibility for their own lives. As social workers realize, there are many prejudgments about oppressed communities. These prejudices are often aimed at the poor, minorities, and other oppressed groups. It is critical for the practitioner to mobilize oppressed people in community change efforts. This can only be accomplished through meaningful participation by these groups in community development.

Resources

As community members involve themselves in change efforts, they often encounter challenges and stress. The practitioner must have the skills to generate the needed resources to help community members who are under pressure as a result of change efforts. Resources of support are not only material but also psychological, such as providing empathy, care, and similar kinds of help for individuals who are under pressure. Providing these kinds of supports to community members involved in change efforts can lead to individual growth and development and ultimately to the responsive community.

Strategy

Strategies based on clear, consistent, and rational expectations must guide the process aimed at changing communities. This kind of information provides community members involved in change efforts with a point of reference and helps ensure that they will act in a coordinated fashion. It is critical for community members involved in community development to have meaningful input to the strategies used for developing the responsive community.

Evaluation

The final aspect of the process aimed at developing the responsive community is to evaluate the change effort. This information is critical because it allows individuals involved in the change process to evaluate the success or failure of their efforts. Furthermore, this information can be used for future efforts in developing responsive community.

CONCLUSION

As noted in this chapter, the community as client is not unlike other clients, such as the small group or organization. The major difference is that the community is a far more complex system to work with than a small group.

Community change efforts must be based on certain strategies critical to the ecological approach to practice. In particular, those who are most affected by change efforts—community members—need to be an intricate part of the planning process. A number of strategies have been introduced to involve community members in this process, including collaborative and task-oriented planning approaches. As the practitioner works with the community, he or she must realize that dysfunctional communities are often closed systems. This kind of system is difficult to work with because it resists change. The practitioner must develop strategies to break through this resistance. This chapter has offered a number of strategies to help the practitioner accomplish this important task.

REFERENCES

Berger, R. L., Federico, R. C., & McBreen, J. T. (1991). *Human behavior: A perspective for the helping professions* (3rd ed.). New York: Longman.

Blocher, D. H., & Biggs, D. A. (1983). *Counseling psychology in community settings.* New York: Springer.

Isoce, I. (1974). Community psychology and the competent community. *American Psychologist, 29*, 607–613.

Watson, G. (1967). Resistance to change. In G. Watson (Ed.), *Concepts for social change* (pp. 10–20). Washington, DC: National Training Laboratories, National Education Association.

Zastrow, C. (1992). *The practice of social work* (4th ed.). Belmont, CA: Wadsworth.

Chapter 3

Individual Intervention: Theories and Techniques

Practitioners at times seem to view their particular theory of individual intervention as a religious faith. Often theories of individual intervention are seen as effective for numerous kinds of problems, even though there is little empirical evidence to support such claims. Social workers grounded in the ecological approach to practice must be aware of the limited evidence supporting the effectiveness of counseling and psychotherapy in general (Eysenck, 1965). The limited empirical support for microlevel intervention approaches should make perfect sense to social workers who assess problems from an ecological perspective. Many psychotherapy and counseling approaches overlook the impact of ecosystems on individual social functioning. They also do not take into account the complex interplay of psychological, social, economic, political, and physical forces on clients. Theories of intervention, such as psychoanalysis, often fail because they do not account for the fact that many problems are the result of the dynamic transaction of the person with his or her environment.

It makes sense from an ecological perspective that inner cities have high crime rates, family breakdown, and other related problems. These kinds of problems are not a symptom of an inner city dweller's inability to control id impulses, as will be argued by a Freudian, but instead are a result of a hostile social environment that does not provide the supports needed for growth and development. Social intervention for the kinds of conditions found in inner cities must be at both the micro- and macrolevels. At the macrolevel, policies and programs need to be implemented that deal with the economic and political problems of the inner city. Thus the effective social worker must become enmeshed in the political process, which can change the political economy and creates a hostile environment for inner city dwellers.

The concept of transaction is also critical to the social practitioner. According to this concept, people are not simply the victims of bad social environments. Individuals, through the transactional process, have a reciprocal relationship with social environment forces. There is a mutual influence between the person and the environment; this unity defines the situation. This means, for example, that those who are trapped by dysfunctional ecosystems can change these systems. The social worker must use his or her knowledge and skills to help clients change such environments. As mentioned in Chapter 2, democratic principles that drive collaborative activities and task-oriented social change are useful strategies for changing the social environment. However, to mobilize people in these kinds of critical activities, the social worker must have both competent macro- and microlevel skills. The effective social worker intervening at both the micro- and macrolevels must be an effective enabler, broker, and mediator.

At times the role of conferee is critical; this is a role that is taken lightly for those involved in traditional psychotherapy and counseling approaches. Thus the effective social work practitioner grounded in an ecological approach is highly skilled in a number of intervention roles. These roles complement each other because all are critical to effective assessment and intervention. It should become clear that the traditional approaches to individual intervention (casework, group work, and community organization) are dated. The effective practitioner uses all three traditional methods in an integrated fashion. It is important, however, for the practitioner to be knowledgeable of the traditional theories of individual intervention, including behavioral, psychosocial, and cognitive. These approaches to intervention can be used effectively with the ecological approach to practice and can be connected to macrolevel assessment and intervention. They help the practitioner understand that ecosystems are comprised of individuals. Behaviors of individuals provide insight into why larger systems behave as they do. Understanding individual action through traditional theories of macrolevel intervention provides a point from which the practitioner can work for social change.

BEHAVIORAL INTERVENTION

Even though there are numerous theorists associated with behavior theory (e.g., Ivan Pavlov and John B. Watson), B. F. Skinner (1953) is the theorist who has had the greatest influence on this orientation to assessment and intervention. Skinner did not develop new principles of behaviorism; instead he translated the theories and ideas of other behaviorists into an applied and useful therapeutic technology. His methods are widely used in psychology, counseling, psychiatry, and social work.

From a behavioral perspective, individuals are viewed as biological entities that respond to the events that happen to them. In essence, people are largely products of their environment. In other words, they are responders to their environments, and these environments shape both functional and dysfunctional behavior.

From an intervention point of view, social workers who use a behavioral approach are grounded in a stimulus–response paradigm. Clients are seen as entities that respond in a predictable fashion to any given stimulus according to what they have learned through past experience. Humans react to stimuli basically in the same fashion as infrahumans, except that human's responses are more organized and complex.

Skinner viewed people as cataloged with a repertoire of responses that are repeated over and over. Specifically, people have learned specific responses that satisfy environmental conditions. This means that individual behavior is very predictable; it also becomes obvious that environmental conditions play a central role in determining behavior. Given this principle, the role of the social worker is one of helping clients unlearn dysfunctional behaviors and replace these with new behaviors. A number of scientifically based principles can assist social workers in helping clients unlearn those behaviors that create problems. Behavioral intervention is a reeducation or relearning process. Positive behaviors are reinforced, and unhelpful behaviors are extinguished. Through reinforcement principles, the client learns functional behavior and unlearns dysfunctional behaviors.

Behavioral intervention involves two types of behavior: operant and respondent. Operant conditioning refers to behavior that operates on and changes the environment in some way. Social workers who use operant conditioning wait until a desired behavior is elicited and then provide positive reinforcement (e.g., praise, free time). Negative reinforcement occurs when the operant behavior is reinforced by its capacity to stop an aversive stimulus. For example, a child will learn to do homework to stop the aversive stimulus—scolding by the child's parents about the child not studying. Extinction is the process of unlearning dysfunctional behavior due to lack of reinforement.

Social workers who do client assessment through behavioral analysis follow these basic steps: (1) Identify the presenting problem, (2) determine the cause of the problem, and (3) select a solution. The solution, or intervention, will involve positive reinforcement of functional behaviors and elimination of undesired behaviors. Some behavioral problems are typically viewed as rooted in antecedents and consequences; these processes thus become the focus of intervention.

A goal of intervention for the social worker is to help the client learn coping strategies. From a philosophical viewpoint, all behavior can be changed—the problem is finding the appropriate positive or negative stimuli to accomplish this goal. Numerous techniques are available to reduce or eliminate anxiety, obsessive behaviors, phobias, depression, and other problematic behaviors (Krumboltz, 1966; Krumboltz & Hosford, 1967). The four main categories for organizing goals of behavioral intervention identified by Krumboltz and Hasford (1967) are:

1. Alerting maladaptive behavior
2. Teaching the decision-making process
3. Preventing problems
4. Teaching new behaviors and skills.

Once a problem is identified, the practitioner can use a variety of counseling techniques to help the client modify behavior to solve a presenting problem. A major goal of behavioral intervention is to teach clients self-management skills they can apply to various life situations. Through this approach, clients learn to become their own behavioral modification experts.

Behaviorists are sensitive to what is referred to as the intraself; however, since this intraself cannot be seen directly, they prefer to work with observable results of these internal psychological processes. The guiding principle behind this position is that if the symptoms can be changed (overt behavior), the internal psychological causes are of secondary importance. In other words, what is critical to the behaviorist is changing those activities that contribute to problems and not necessarily their cause.

There are a number of techniques that social workers can employ when using behavioral intervention. These include contingency contracting, self-management, shaping, biofeedback, and modeling. The following is an example of contingency contracting, which involves five steps:

1. Identify the problem.
2. Collect baseline data with which to understand events associated with the problem.
3. Set goals to solve the problem.
4. Select techniques for obtaining the goals.
5. If goals are not reached, establish new behavioral change strategies.

The process is clearly grounded in science; furthermore, a single-subject methodology neatly fits this approach.

Self-management is a strategy that helps clients learn how to take control of their lives. The major difference between self-management and other behavioral approaches is that the client assumes responsibility for changing behavior. The intervention process includes the following steps:

1. Define the problem in behavioral terms.
2. Collect data on the problem.
3. Introduce a treatment plan based on behavioral principles.
4. Evaluate the plan.
5. If the plan is not working, change it.

There are numerous self-management books and manuals available to help clients change problem behaviors (Pardeck, 1994).

Shaping is an operant technique to induce new behaviors by reinforcing ones that approximate the desired behavior. Through this process, the client gradually achieves the designed behavior. The technique involves the social worker's (1) looking, (2) waiting, and (3) reinforcing during intervention. In other words, the practitioner waits for the client to exhibit positive behavior and then reinforces it. Through this shaping process, the client gradually develops functional behaviors.

Biofeedback uses a machine versus a practitioner to shape behavior. Monitoring, through machine technology, can help the client learn to develop more desirable behaviors. Machine technologies presently available can monitor muscle tension, brain waves, heart rate, and other responses, which are fed back to the client through auditory and visual means. The more the client relaxes, the slower the beeping sounds on the monitor become. Through this process, the client gradually learns behaviors that contribute to his or her total well-being.

Modeling is another helpful technique for shaping behavior. This approach uses people, books, videotapes, and other resources to teach functional behaviors. The practitioner may also serve as a model. A goal of modeling is to help the client gain awareness of how his or her behavior is controlled and shaped by the environment. The following steps are an example of how videotaping can be used through modeling:

1. The client identifies behaviors that he or she wishes to change.
2. Through videotaping, the practitioner gathers baseline data associated with the undesirable behavior.
3. The practitioner offers other models through videotape that illustrate more desirable behavior.
4. The client practices these new positive behaviors while being videotaped and gradually learns the desired behaviors.

Exposure to positive models has been effective regardless of whether the model or the observer receives visible reinforcement.

The literature offers numerous approaches one can use for conducting behavioral approaches (see, e.g., Pardeck, 1994). It is also noted that behavioral approaches are valid and widely applicable to the various clinical problems that social workers treat. What is also important is that research strongly supports the behavioral approach; in other words, the approach works. Behaviorist theorists were the first to mount a significant attack on psychodynamic models that were widely used prior to the behavioral approach's development. Social workers who use a behavioral approach work with phenomena that are empirically based; such a strategy allows one to document effectiveness in practice.

PSYCHODYNAMIC INTERVENTION

Theorists who represent the psychodynamic approach to therapy include Freud, Jung, Alder, and Erikson. Since the founding of Freudianism, numerous books and articles have been written about the psychodynamic approach to treatment. Even though many of the ideas associated with this approach have been challenged and criticized as lacking empirical evidence, psychodynamic theorists have heavily influenced modern-day clinical intervention.

A psychodynamic orientation views the individual as a being strongly influenced by psychic determinism and unconscious mental processes. Psychic determinism suggests that emotional life is guided by a preordained process grounded in instincts and drives. Moreover, behavior is largely a result of unconscious mental processes often unrecognized by the person. These unconscious processes include feelings that result in repression and anxiety and cause conflict within the self. The goal of therapy is to help the person gain insight into the unconscious self and thus increase self-understanding and development.

The parts of the personality as defined by Freud—the id, ego, and superego—are found in various forms in psychodynamic theory. For example, Erikson (1963) used all three terms in his theory of personality; however, he redefined what each concept meant. The following sections define each concept of the parts of the personality as originally created by Freud.

Id

This part of the personality is composed of basic instinctual drives: hunger, thirst, and aggression. Freud concluded that the id is a pleasure-seeking part of the personality that demands immediate gratification. The id seeks gratification regardless of consequences.

Ego

The ego is understood to be the part of the personality that negotiates a balance between the id and superego. It is reality oriented, rational, and operates under the reality principle. It is the thinking part of the personality.

Superego

This aspect of the personality is composed of general moral principles that guide the ego. The therapist must help the troubled individual work through this conflict resulting from moral principles.

Freudian therapy includes a number of concepts that help one understand better how the personality works in the individual (e.g., instinct, libido, and anxiety). According to Freud, instinct is an inborn need that flows from the physiological condition referred to as a need. Thirst is a need that can be understood as a life instinct. Libido is the force that provides energy aimed at meeting basic needs. Anxiety refers to a painful internal psychological process that creates fear in the individual. Neurotic anxiety, for example, results from a fear of one's instinctual drives flowing from the id, and the ego's function is to help control this process.

Psychodynamic theory has been influenced by the developmental concepts of what Freud labeled as defense mechanisms. These are essentially strategies used by the ego to protect the person from various internal psychological turmoil (Clark, 1991). Examples of defense mechanisms include the following.

Projection

Projection is a process by which the person attributes his or her own characteristics to others. A social worker, for example, may feel uncomfortable admitting that he or she does not like the elderly. Instead the practitioner uses projection by suggesting that the elderly do not like him or her.

Rationalization

When using this form of defense mechanism, the person uses a rational reason for dealing with failure. This reason may not be consistent with reality; however, it is a strategy for justifying one's action. The typical form of rationalization is to blame others for one's failure.

Withdrawal

This process involves a strategy of avoiding those situations that may hurt the person. For example, one learns to reduce ego involvement by withdrawing from relationships that are seen as risky.

Displacement

When individuals use displacement as a means of coping, they redirect their energy from a primary object. For example, a child may become angry at a parent, but displacement occurs when the child redirects the anger at the family cat.

Many therapists use defense mechanisms as concepts for helping clients understand their actions. A psychodynamic approach to treatment suggests that everyone uses these processes to protect the self. People only become dysfunctional when they distort reality to such a degree that they can no longer cope effectively.

A final important concept in Freudian theory is catharsis. Modern-day psychodynamic theorists continue to use this concept in treatment. It is grounded in the position that many traumatic life events are pushed to the unconscious. The result is dysfunctional behavior that makes little sense to the person because it is triggered by the unconscious. If this repressed information is not brought to the awareness of the conscious self, problem behaviors continue. A goal of therapy is to help a client develop insight into repressed past psychological trauma. By doing so, the client has a cathartic experience that helps relieve psychological pain. This can be accomplished through verbalization and the emotional reliving of a past painful experience. This pronouncement is guided through talk therapy; in essence, the dialogue between the practitioner and client is the core medium through which therapy takes place.

Payne (1991) summarizes the numerous criticisms of psychodynamic theory:

1. As a theory, it lacks empirical verification.
2. Psychodynamic theory has a tendency to reinforce stereotypes of women as domestics and intellectually inferior to men.
3. People are referred to as patients; thus psychodynamic theory operates from a medical model orientation.
4. Psychodynamic theory makes cultural assumptions that are unfounded in social science.
5. After insight is gained into a presenting problem, psychodynamic theory does not offer solutions to solving the problem.
6. Clients who are not verbally able to express problems find little benefit in psychodynamic therapy.
7. Environmental factors are almost entirely overlooked as a source for psychological problems. Thus the clinician starts with a very narrow set of assumptions about the origin of client problems.
8. The political, social, and cultural contexts of clients are overlooked, thus excluding important information from the assessment and intervention process. This results in limited therapeutic success.

Even though there are numerous limitations to psychodynamic theory, it is an important orientation because it is the basis for modern-day social intervention. This distinction suggests that practitioners must study the psychodynamic tradition to gain better insight into holistic theories, such as the ecological approach to assessment and intervention.

COGNITIVE THERAPEUTIC INTERVENTION

The focus of cognitive therapy is on psychological disturbances caused by aberrations in thinking. The role of the therapist is to help clients develop psychological skills to correct this condition. These skills include labeling and interpreting negative psychological disturbances and ultimately correcting these conditions through therapy. Practitioners must realize that cognitive therapy demands that clients have the capacity for introspection and reflecting on their thoughts and feelings. These activities are aimed at increasing client self-awareness, and the goal of this process is for clients to substitute accurate judgments for inaccurate ones. Not all clients have the cognitive or intellectual capacity to engage in this form of therapy (Ellis, 1975).

A number of therapists represent the cognitive therapeutic approach, including A. Beck (1976), William Glasser (1969), and Albert Ellis (1975). The focus of this discussion will be on Ellis, clearly the leading figure in the field of cognitive therapy. Ellis views human beings as largely irrational beings that need to be taught rational approaches for dealing with problems. Humans think crookedly about their desires and preferences, thus resulting in anger, anxiety, depression, and self-pity. Unfortunately, irrational thinking leads to self-hate, which may lead to self-destructive behavior and eventually to hatred of others.

Ellis (1975) believes that some irrational thoughts are biological in origin, but most result from the socialization process. The following list illustrates what individuals tell themselves when they interpret events in an irrational fashion. In these examples, a more rational thought follows the irrational message (Thompson & Rudolph, 1992, pp. 134–135).

1. It is preferable that I be outstandingly competent; I absolutely must be this way, and if not I am awful and worthless. Rational thought alternative: It would be nice to be outstanding and competent, but if I am not, that is still okay.

2. Because it is highly desirable that others treat me fairly, if they do not, they must be rotten. Rational thought alternative: I would prefer people to treat me kindly; however, I realize this is not always the case. I will not take it personally when they treat me poorly, and I will make it my business to be considerate.

3. Because it is preferable that I experience pleasure rather than pain, the world should arrange this condition for me; life is horrible if the world does not create this condition. Rational thought alternative: I realize in real life there are pleasurable moments and painful moments; consequently, I will try to make painful moments positive learning experiences that I can benefit from.

Theory of Intervention

Thompson and Rudolph (1992, pp. 135–136) offer a number of irrational beliefs that cause people trouble. These are based on the work of Ellis and include the following:

1. It is a necessity for me to be loved by everyone in whatever I do.
2. People should be thoroughly competent, adequate, and achieving in all possible respects.
3. Certain individuals are wicked, and they should be punished for their wickedness.
4. It is terrible and horrible when things are not going well for me.
5. Unhappiness is externally caused; people have little or no ability to control sorrow or rid themselves of their negative feelings.
6. If something is dangerous, one must be terribly occupied with this danger.
7. It is easier to avoid life difficulties than to attempt to face them.
8. The past is all important and strongly affects one's life; this never changes in the future.
9. People should be different, and it is catastrophic if perfect solutions to problems are not found immediately.
10. Maximum human happiness can be achieved by inertia and inaction.
11. My terrible childhood has caused me to be a failure as a parent.
12. I cannot as a parent give my children everything; therefore I am a failure.

Thompson and Rudolph (1992, p. 136) list a number of consequences that may result from irrational thinking:

1. Interpersonal difficulties
2. Emotionalism as a way of reacting to daily problems
3. Fixation on what one cannot have

4. Not appreciating what one has
5. Seeing oneself as worthless
6. Attributing one's difficulties to others
7. Behavior that is inconsistent with one's goals
8. Tolerating negative situations by not taking steps to correct them
9. Remaining dependent on others when one does not need to
10. Remaining angry or hurt beyond a reasonable period of time
11. Demanding perfection in others and self
12. Indulging in behavior that damages the mind and body
13. Unreasonable fears
14. Excessive behavior.

The goal of rational-emotive therapy is to teach people to think and behave in a more functional fashion. Furthermore, people must take responsibility for the self, including their own logical thinking and the behaviors that result from their thinking. By teaching clients to reflect on their thinking, practitioners can correct the kind of thinking that results in those consequences.

CONCLUSION

An ecological perspective views the assessment process in a holistic fashion (i.e., presenting problems are assessed at both the micro- and macrolevels). The goal of intervention is to treat not only the microlevel aspects of a presenting problem but also the macrolevel components. Theories of intervention aimed at changing individuals are covered in this chapter. These theories should be viewed as useful strategies for assessing and treating the microlevel aspects of an ecological approach to practice.

The two individual-based theories that have the greatest utility for assessing and treating problems from an ecological view are behaviorism and cognitive therapeutic intervention; both of these intervention strategies have been shown to be highly effective (Thompson & Rudolph, 1992). Furthermore, both intervention approaches are theoretically connected to an ecological perspective.

A behavioral approach is particularly powerful from an ecological point of view because of its emphasis on the environment in shaping individual behavior, a view clearly aligned with an ecological orientation. However, an ecological approach does depart significantly from behavioral theory in that humans are seen as organisms that affect the larger ecology or social environment; behaviorists do not hold such a view. Regardless of this theoretical difference, behavioral techniques can be used as effective intervention strategies by social workers grounded in an ecological approach.

Cognitive therapeutic intervention can also be a useful approach supporting an ecological perspective. As ecological theorists stress, the transactional process is the focal point of treatment. Cognitive techniques can be used as strategies to help clients improve their transactions with the ecosystems encompassing their social environments. For example, parents who are having interpersonal difficulties with a child who is not living up to their expectations must be taught rational approaches to dealing with their youngster. Parents who demand perfection are probably approaching their children from an irrational perspective, and this irrationality creates a transactional process between parents and child that results in dysfunctional behavior. Practitioners grounded in an ecological approach, for example, will help parents demanding perfection in their child reflect on their thinking processes that lead to such demands. The goal of treatment in such cases would be to help parents rethink their approaches for dealing with the child; once this goal is accomplished, the transactional process between parents and child should improve for the better. There are countless problems that can be corrected if cognitive therapy is used to help clients change their transactions with the various systems encompassing their social environments.

Psychodynamic approaches—treatment strategies that largely emphasize the intrapsychic in both assessment and treatment—appear to have limited utility for social workers grounded in an ecological orientation to intervention. Concepts such as psychic determinism seem to disregard the importance of environment in shaping one's behavior. The overemphasis on pathology in psychodynamic therapies strongly suggests that they are grounded in the medical model. As stressed in Chapter 1, theories that rely on the medical model often have limited utility because of a narrow, often one-dimensional view of cause, and in general they have great potential for dehumanizing clients. However, social workers grounded in the ecological approach must realize that modern-day therapies (such as cognitive therapy) have historical roots in the psychodynamic approaches. Furthermore, many modern-day therapeutic approaches are grounded in the psychodynamic tradition, so this tradition must be appreciated.

Behavioral and cognitive therapeutic approaches appear to be the most useful strategies for enhancing an ecological approach to practice. They are also strategies that can be used to help clients alter their transactions with their larger social environments.

REFERENCES

Beck, A. (1976). *Cognitive therapy and emotional disorder*. New York: International Universities Press.

Clark, A. (1991). The identification and modification of defense mechanism in counseling. *Journal of Counseling and Development, 63,* 231–236.

Ellis, A. (1975). The impossibility of achieving consistently good mental health. *American Psychologist, 42,* 364–375.

Erikson, E. (1963). *Childhood and society*. New York: Norton.

Eysenck, H. J. (1965). The effects of psychotherapy. *International Journal of Psychiatry, 1,* 97–144.

Glasser, W. (1969). *The identity society*. New York: Harper & Row.

Krumboltz, J. (1966). Behavioral counseling. *Journal of Counseling Psychology, 13,* 153–159.

Krumboltz, J., & Hosford, R. (1967). Behavioral counseling in the elementary school. *Elementary School Guidance and Counseling, 1,* 27–40.

Pardeck, J. T. (1994). *Using bibliotherapy in clinical practice: A guide to self-help books*. Westport, CT: Greenwood Press.

Payne, M. (1991). *Modern social work theory: A critical introduction*. Chicago: Lyceum.

Skinner, B. F. (1953). *Science and human behavior*. New York: Macmillan.

Thompson, C. L., & Rudolph, L. B. (1992). *Counseling children* (3rd ed.). Pacific Grove, CA: Brooks/Cole.

Chapter 4

Group Work from an Ecological Perspective

Social workers grounded in an ecological approach view the human group as an important system that affects the social functioning of individuals. Groups are defined as a multiperson system that encompasses the interaction between two or more people. Examples of multiperson systems include recreational, educational, therapeutic, and personal growth groups. The family is a special case of the multiperson system because it includes primary group relationships that are long term. These qualities are not found in other small group systems. Intervention with the family group is the major emphasis in this chapter.

As many practitioners realize, the term *group* is imprecise and can include many kinds of multiperson systems. Johnson's (1995, p. 193) definition for the small group is clearly grounded in the ecological perspective, and practitioners will find it a useful orientation to understanding group systems. She defines the group as "a social system comprised of two or more persons who have something in common and who use face-to-face interaction to share commonalty and work to fulfill common needs and solve common problems, their own and others." Groups have boundaries that separate them from other systems. They have relationships that include roles that fulfill needs of group members. Groups include bonds that hold members together. Finally, group functioning is a complex process influenced by the actions and interactions of group members.

TRADITIONAL GROUP INTERVENTION

Traditional group approaches include recreational, educational, therapeutic, and personal growth groups. The following sections summarize the nature of these kinds of groups.

Recreational Groups

The goal of this kind of group is pure enjoyment. Recreational groups often do not have leaders, and activities are typically spontaneous. Examples of these kinds of groups include playground and game room activities and informal baseball, volleyball, or football groups. The recreational group is often viewed as a system that prevents juvenile groups (i.e., gangs) and builds character.

Educational Groups

The goal of this kind of small group system is to help participants acquire knowledge and learn complex skills. Leaders of this form of group are well trained and are often professionals. Educational groups focus on a variety of topics, including training foster parents, teaching parenting techniques, and training volunteers for specialized functions with human service systems. Social workers are often leaders of educational groups. When working with educational groups, social workers encourage discussion and in-depth group interaction.

Therapeutic Groups

Group therapy is an advanced form of group work that attempts to deal with unconscious motivation and personality changes of participants. Group therapy is often of long-term duration and includes clients with severe emotional disabilities. It is conducted in schools, institutions, and mental health centers. Social workers leading group therapy are highly trained professionals grounded in advanced knowledge and skills in small group interaction.

Personal Growth Groups

This form of group is often composed of healthy people who wish to improve their lives. They seek to improve communication skills, develop leadership skills, improve relationship skills, and develop the personal attitudes or abilities of group members. They attempt to encourage growth by helping group members reassess their potential and act positively on this reassessment. Classic examples of personal growth groups include the encounter group (Coulson, 1970; Rogers, 1970) and integrity groups (Mowrer, 1972).

Of the aforementioned groups, all but the recreational group rely on group leaders. Consequently, group leaders become critical to the positive functioning of many group situations. Cartwright (1951) identifies eight principles based on group dynamics that social workers may find helpful in facilitating group functioning:

1. Groups will only be successful as a medium of change if people who are to change can exert influence for change and have a feeling of belongingness.

2. The greater the attractiveness of the group to the person, the greater the influence of the group on members.

3. When attempting to change attitudes, values, or behaviors of group members, the more relevant these factors are to the group, the greater the influence they have on members.

4. The greater the prestige of a group member in the eyes of other members, the greater the influence he or she will have on the group.

5. Efforts aimed at changing group members are often successful by pressuring the person to conform to group norms and standards. The deviant group member must realize that deviation will result in rejection or expulsion.

6. Strong pressures aimed at change can be established by creating a shared perception among group members of the need for change; thus the pressure for change comes from within the group.

7. Information that focuses on the need for change must be shared by all relevant group members.

8. Change in one part of the group can produce stress in other parts of the group; this process can only be eliminated by reducing change efforts or by bringing about readjustment in the related parts.

All of these principles can be used as effective strategies by group leaders to improve group functioning. Practitioners assessing and treating problems from an ecological perspective will find these principles useful for analyzing group functioning.

FAMILY THERAPY

Family therapy is a relatively new and innovative treatment that is clearly grounded in the ecological perspective. It is a highly useful technique for practitioners because virtually all clients are connected to family systems. Other group intervention approaches, such as the therapeutic group, have more narrow goals because they deal with unique problems and specialized people. Family therapists, when working with clients experiencing problems, always have the client's family present or pictured in the therapist's thoughts during treatment. This orientation is shared by virtually all family therapists regardless of their theoretical perspective (Pardeck, 1989).

The orientation that dominates family therapy is systems theory. Foley (1974) suggests that one cannot read any of the major family theorists without having extensive knowledge of systems theory and how this perspective applies to the family. The emphasis on systems theory has revolutionized how individual pathology is viewed. Pathology from a systems perspective moves pathology away from the individual to the family systems level. Even though family therapy was initially rejected by many mental health professionals in the 1950s and 1960s, most mental health professionals now see it as an intricate part of treatment (Pardeck, 1981).

The communicative-integrative approach to family therapy should be viewed as the family treatment approach of choice for practitioners using an ecological approach. Other orientations to family therapy include a traditional psychoanalytic approach (Framo, 1965) and integrative family treatment (Foley, 1974). These two approaches do not place the same level of emphasis on systems theory as the communicative-integrative approach. Virginia Satir and Jay Haley are the family therapists who have contributed the theoretical grounding to the communicative-integrative approach (Pardeck, 1981).

Satir and Haley best represent the communicative-integrative orientation to family therapy for a number of reasons. Neither view the individual as the focus of treatment. In contrast, psychoanalytic family treatment incorporates psychoanalysis as the major grounding principle for intervention. Psychic determinism and the subconscious mind, among other Freudian ideas, are important to the psychoanalytic family therapist.

As would be expected, the systems approach is not stressed among psychoanalytic family therapists. For example, Boszormenyi-Nagy and Framo, both psychoanalytic family therapists, stress the unconscious dynamics of family members and other Freudian concepts. Neither therapist emphazizes systems theory (Pardeck, 1981). In fact, Framo (1965) suggests that family members cannot undergo significant and meaningful change unless the therapist deals with the most powerful obstacle to successful treatment: the individual member's libidinal attachments to parental introjects, no matter what the parents were like in real life. Consequently, the focus on the individual family member over the family system opens this orientation to the same criticisms of treatment that focuses only on the individual (Pardeck, 1981).

The final dominant therapeutic approach to family therapy is the integrative approach. Nathan Ackerman was the leading advocate of this approach until his death. Ackerman stressed that the family encompasses the interdependent, interpenetrating relations of the individual and the family system (Foley, 1974, p. 55). He suggested that treatment should not pit the individual over the family or the family over the individual; in essence, both units are critical to the treatment process. Pardeck (1981) suggests that the integrative approach is the bridge between the psychoanalytic and communicative-integrative approaches to family therapy. Furthermore, Ackerman felt that total acceptance of a systems family therapy perspective was not possible.

FAMILY-CENTERED THERAPY

The communicative-integrative family therapy approach is clearly the treatment perspective most aligned with the ecological perspective. One obvious indication of this alignment is that the communicative-integrative approach is almost entirely divorced from traditional psychological theories. For example, the personality is mainly conceptualized as a result of social interaction. Thus such traditional concepts as psychic determinism, individual pathology, the medical model, defense mechanisms, and so on are not relevant to the communicative-integrative approach. The core strategy for understanding families through this approach is analyzing the communication processes among family members. This approach stresses communication in two ways: (1) the ways in which messages are sent and received within the family unit and (2) the paths of communication within the family system (Pardeck, 1981). As would be expected, communication is a core medium of the transactional process and is a focal point of the assessment and intervention process when using the ecological approach.

The communicative-integrative approach to treating problems stresses that the first priority of the therapist is to promote an adaptive, need-fulfilling balance between the family and surrounding ecosystems. Since this approach to family therapy is heavily grounded in systems theory, the larger social environment in which the family system functions is an intricate part of the treatment process.

As noted earlier, Haley and Satir are the two therapists who best represent the communicative-interactive approach. Their position on social intervention heavily integrates ecological concepts. Haley (1977), for example, suggests that many treatment modalities are not successful because they do not take into account the impact of social systems on individual functioning. He suggests that practitioners who define presenting problems from a psychodynamic perspective often neglect important information that is grounded in the ecosystems of clients. Haley elaborates in great length on why pathology is located in the family or larger social ecology and not the individual. In essence, Haley feels that people's problems are found in social forces and that these forces shape and mold the individual.

Satir (1967) also de-emphasizes individual-based treatment. She argues that therapy must be conducted in the context of the family system. Satir, clearly in the sociological tradition, feels that one's self-concept is a product of multiple relationships with various systems. This position is a rejection of traditional individual-based treatments and is well beyond the boundaries of the medical model for assessment and treatment.

MINUCHIN'S FAMILY FUNCTIONING MODEL

Salvador Minuchin (1974), a family therapist, has developed a dynamic model of family functioning that connects family treatment to the ecological perspective. Minuchin argues that the family system is in continual transition; given this process, it is constantly adapting and accommodating to new situations. If the family is not able to adapt and accommodate to these transitions, problems will emerge for the family system as well as individual family members. What is dynamic about Minuchin's model is its grounding in the ecological theoretical tradition. That is, pressures on families emerge from within and outside the family during various transition points. This means that practitioners who work with families must treat not only pressures emerging from the family unit but also factors external to the family and flowing from the social environment.

Minuchin's (1974) model is powerful because it helps the practitioner anchor the self in the ecological perspective and understand that pressure on families comes from four sources (discussed shortly). Minuchin makes it clear that the family's movements through various transition points of development are predictable and that most families experience the same pressures.

The first source of pressure on the family unit flows from forces on one family member. When a family member is under pressure, that individual's interaction and transaction with other family members may result in problems that permeate the entire family system. An example might be a wife who is under pressure at work; when she arrives home from work she criticizes her husband, and the result of this transaction may be a family fight. The fight can be resolved by positive closure and mutual support, or it may evolve into new pressures on the family. Obviously, the skills of each family member will determine if there is positive or negative closure to the pressures on the family system emerging from one member. However, the problem could be corrected more easily if the stressed family member experiences improved work conditions. If this correction is made in the stressed family member's ecosystem—the workplace—this source of pressure on the family system would be alleviated.

Pearlin and Schooler (1978) have identified a number of psychological resources that can help family members deal with extrafamilial pressures on individual family members. These are critical because at times the extrafamilial pressures cannot be changed, and thus the family system must develop coping mechanisms to deal with the external pressure. One factor, the self-esteem of individual family members, can have a significant impact on how families cope with extrafamilial stress. Specifically, family members with high self-esteem can enhance a family system's mechanisms for coping with external family pressures. The individual family member's attitude about the external world—that is, his or her feeling of mastery of external events and his or her interpersonal communication skills—is critical to family functioning. Morris and Engle (1981) add that the individual family member's coping styles and efforts are important in helping family members deal with external family pressure.

Another source of extrafamilial pressure are forces that affect the entire family system. These sources include economic pressures (e.g., poverty) and the pressure created when a family moves to a new neighborhood or must deal with the overload created by the numerous social service agencies that help poverty-stricken families cope with economic pressures.

Minuchin (1974) argues that pressure also occurs as a family moves through its life cycle. These pressures are typical in most families; however, not all families cope with them effectively. For example, when parents have their first child, tremendous pressures emerge within the family system. Specifically, there is a readjustment of family roles and, in general, power shifts occur within the family. Some families cannot cope with these pressures and will need social treatment. Other families adapt to and accommodate the changes brought about by the entry of a child into the family system. Throughout the life cycle of the family, various pressures emerge at different transition points of family development. These stages are not stress free and at times will have to be treated with social intervention.

The final source of stress on the family system emerges from idiosyncratic problems unique to various families. For example, families that have children with disabilities often have limited problems as long as the children are at home; however, once special children move into the educational system, the families have problems coping with that transition. Another idiosyncratic problem occurs when a family member become seriously ill. The seriously ill family member's functioning and power within the family unit change, and the entire system must readjust. Some families do not cope with this kind of readjustment in a functional fashion. Then, in turn, when the family member recovers from the serious illness, the family system must realign itself.

In sum, Minuchin's model helps the practitioner understand that treatment of the family group must not only include work with individual family members but also work with the larger social ecology that often creates pressures on the family system. Furthermore, the practitioner who is grounded in the ecological perspective realizes that the quality of social policy aimed at the family system can have a major effect on family functioning (Pardeck, 1982). For example, Kamerman and Kahn (1978) have illustrated in their work on family policy that many family problems in American society would be eliminated if the United States had a coordinated, comprehensive family policy. The underdevelopment of family policy in the United States has resulted in extensive poverty, child abuse, and neglect as well as a host of related problems. Simply put, many of the sources of pressure on family systems identified in Minuchin's model would be eradicated if there were programs available to help families adapt to and accommodate extrafamilial pressures. Since these programs are virtually nonexistent, an important part of the social worker's practice is to advocate for quality family programs. These macrolevel efforts have the potential to improve the ecosystems that transact with the family system and ultimately help determine the quality of family life and functioning.

ECOLOGICAL APPROACH AND GROUP INTERVENTION

The ecological perspective stresses the importance of the individual's relationship with his or her social environment. This orientation argues that individuals are shaped and molded by their social environment and that groups, including the family group, play a critical role in this process. This development has redefined how practitioners in the human services field assess and treat presenting problems of clients.

Middleman and Goldberg (1974), both social work theorists, have influenced this movement toward an ecological approach to practice through their structural approach to social intervention. They conclude that problems of clients are found in the social environment and not necessarily in clients. Furthermore, they reject theory and treatment methods that isolate problems of people within the person, not the social environment. These rejected treatments, not surprisingly, include psychoanalysis and other related medical models for therapy. The basis to Middleman and Goldberg's theory can be found in the disciplines of psychology and sociology, both of which have developed strong theories that the social environment plays a critical role in a person's social functioning (Pardeck, 1981). Within the field of psychology, this includes behavioral theorists; the discipline of sociology has been focusing on the forces of the social environment on the person since the nineteenth century. Warshay (1975), a sociologist, defines the ecological perspective from a sociological view:

It is a perspective which is essentially focused at the macro level; it heavily emphasizes the role of the social environment on communities, social organizations, social groups, and the individual. It is a perspective which de-emphasizes the psychological and other micro level perspectives. (pp. 43–44)

This definition illustrates the synthesis of ecological theory with the fields of sociology and social work. Practitioners using the ecological approach to practice would not feel uncomfortable with Warshay's definition.

CONCLUSION

An ecological perspective helps practitioners work more effectively with all kinds of groups. The major emphasis in this chapter, however, illustrates effective ecological-based practice with families. The form of family treatment that receives the greatest emphasis in this chapter is the communicative-interactive approach, an intervention aligned with the ecological perspective.

The communicative-interactive approach to family treatment is based on assumptions also found within ecological theory. For example, both perspectives stress the importance of the social environment on the individual. Each perspective suggests that social problems confronting people have a major impact on individual social functioning. Furthermore, traditional psychological approaches, particularly the medical model, provide little insight into individual social functioning because presenting problems are not viewed as flowing from one's transactions and interactions with one's social environment, but instead from one's biological self.

As a group intervention technique, the communicative-interactive approach appears to be the most useful approach for working with families. Haley (1973) argues that the communicative-interactive orientation is powerful because practitioners who use it work not only in the office but also in the business place, on the street, in the school, and in the client's home. Haley also suggests that practitioners, when working with the family group, need to think in structural terms and about how these structures (such as the school and neighborhood) affect family and individual social functioning. The following quote from Haley (1973) summarizes eloquently why the communicative-interactive approach generally is a powerful technique for working with families:

What family therapists most have in common they also share with a number of behavioral scientists in the world today; there is an increasing awareness that psychiatric problems are social problems which involve the total ecological system. There is a concern with, and an attempt to change, what happens with the family, its interlocking systems, and the social institutions in which it is imbedded. The fragmentation of the individual, or the family, into parts is being abandoned. There is a growing consensus that a new ecological framework defines problems in new ways, and calls for new ways in therapy. (pp. 166–167)

REFERENCES

Cartwright, D. (1951). Achieving change in people: Some complications of group dynamics theory. *Human Relations, 4*, 381–393.

Coulson, W. (1970). Inside a basic encounter group. *The Counseling Psychologist, 2*, 1–27.

Foley, V. D. (1974). *An introduction to family therapy.* New York: Grune &
       Stratton.
Framo, J. L. (1965). Rationale and techniques of intensive family therapy.
       In I. Boszormenyi-Nagy & J. Framo (Eds.), *Intensive family ther-
       apy* (pp. 50–61). New York: Harper & Row.
Haley, J. (1973). *The book of family therapy.* Boston: Houghton Mifflin.
———. (1977). *Problem-solving therapy.* San Francisco, CA: Jossey-Bass.
Johnson, L. C. (1995). *Social work practice: A generalist approach* (5th ed.).
       Needham Heights, MA: Allyn & Bacon.
Kamerman, S. B., & Kahn. A. J. (1978). *Family policy.* New York: Columbia
       University Press.
Middleman, R., & Goldberg, G. (1974). *Social service delivery: A structural
       approach to social work practice.* New York: Columbia University
       Press.
Minuchin, S. (1974). *Families and family therapy.* Boston: MA: Harvard
       University Press.
Morris, L. W., & Engle, W. B. (1981). Assessing various coping strategies
       and their effects on test performance and anxiety. *Journal of
       Clinical Psychology, 37,* 165–171.
Mowrer, O. H. (1972). Integrity groups: Basic principles and objectives.
       The Counseling Psychologist, 3, 4–6.
Pardeck, J. T. (1981). The current state and new direction of family ther-
       apy. *Family Therapy, 8,* 113–120.
———. (1982). Family policy: An ecological approach supporting family
       therapy treatment. *Family Therapy, 9,* 163–165.
———. (1989). Family therapy as a treatment approach to child abuse.
       Family Therapy, 16, 113–120.
Pearlin, L., & Schooler, C. (1978). The structure of coping. *Journal of Health
       and Social Behavior, 19,* 2–21.
Rogers, C. R. (1970). *Carl Rogers on encounter groups.* New York: Harper &
       Row.
Satir, V. (1967). *Conjoint family therapy.* Palo Alto, CA: Science and Behav-
       ior Books.
Warshay, L. H. (1975). *The current state of sociological theory.* New York:
       McKay.

Chapter 5

Consultation and Training

Consultation is becoming a critical activity among professional social workers. It is an important role for social workers using an ecological approach to practice because it is a professional role aimed at providing guidance to agencies and organizations focusing on strategies that help increase the effectiveness and efficiency of services. In essence, it deals with the micro, mezzo, and macro aspects of social work intervention and has the ultimate goal of improving services to clients.

The field of community psychology offers a highly developed knowledge base that focuses on consultation and that social workers will find useful (Blocher & Biggs, 1983). Specifically, the field of community psychology divides consultation into two forms: triadic and process. Triadic consultation is a process in which the consultant offers indirect helping, whereas process consultation involves direct work with an organization with the aim of improving services. The following discussion focuses on these two approaches to consultation.

Triadic consultation is a process of providing indirect help, mainly through the role of mediator, to those practitioners involved in direct service delivery to clients. The practitioner involved in the triadic approach to consultation works with a variety of helping professionals, including other social workers, teachers, psychologists, and related human services personnel. When doing triadic consultation, the practitioner attempts to help others improve their services. Treatment success under these conditions is judged by how effective the direct practitioner was in the delivery of services to a client after receiving consultation (Blocher & Biggs, 1983, p. 117).

Process consultation involves working with a complex social system with the aim of improving its functioning. The complex social system that the practitioner works with would be an entire organization or a subpart of a larger organization. This is clearly a macrolevel form of intervention and suggests that a practitioner must have a clear understanding of how complex organizations work and, more importantly, how one changes larger systems when they are not functioning well.

The process consultation role includes such activities as helping an agency improve its policies and procedures used in the delivery of services. Specifically, it may involve helping an agency realize the differences between efficiency and effectiveness and gain insight into the consequences for organization life when a system emphasizes one over the other. For example, computer technology has great potential to improve the efficiency of an agency at all levels; however, the consequence of this may be that the effectiveness of services delivery decreases. Some practitioners even argue that the efficiency that emerges from the use of computer technology in an agency setting may be dehumanizing to both clients and workers (Murphy & Pardeck, 1991). Clearly, practitioners using an ecological approach to practice will be heavily involved in both triadic and process consultation because of their emphasis on changing macrolevel systems.

LEVELS OF FOCUS

Blocher and Biggs (1983) suggest that there are three levels of consultation: technical, collaborative, and facilitative. The nature of the problem facing the practitioner will determine which level of consultation is called for.

Consultation at the technical level occurs when the practitioner provides expert opinion, direction, and information concerning a specific problem. This level of consultation is specific and narrow because it emphasizes the needs of an organization and how these needs can be better met.

The collaborative level of consultation stresses the interaction and cooperation between complex systems. The consultant may be a member of one system, and the consultee is involved in another system. An example of this might be the consultant who is working for a family services agency; he or she helps the consultee, a school system, improve educational and services delivery to students. The collaborative level of consultation involves sharing information, planning, evaluating, and performing other activities that improve collaboration between systems (Blocher & Biggs, 1983, p. 125).

The final level of consultation is facilitative. This level of consulting involves a professional from outside the organization who is brought into a system with the goal of improving system functioning. Specifically, the focus may be on organizational structure, interpersonal relationships, or other processes critical to optimal organizational functioning. To be successful in consultation at this level, one must have excellent skills in assessing and working with those aspects of organizational life that either inhibit or facilitate the functioning of large systems.

Blocher and Biggs (1983) conclude that effective practitioners must be able to do consultation at all three levels—technical, collaborative, and facilitative. They also stress that each of these consultation strategies is not necessarily mutually exclusive and may be done jointly. The nature of an organizational problem will determine the consulting levels at which the practitioner will intervene.

AN APPROACH TO CONSULTATION

Consultation needs to be well-conceived to be effective. The following steps can be used to achieve effective consultation. This model is based on the work of Blocher and Biggs (1983) and has gone through significant modification to conform to the field of social work. It can be used with micro (individuals and groups) and macro (organizational) systems.

Stage One: Defining Goals and Objectives

Once the practitioner has been invited to offer consultation, it is critical to help the system he or she is working with establish clear goals and objectives for change. Often, those who seek consultation have unrealistic goals and objectives for meeting the needs of an organization. An important initial step for the consultant is to help an organization establish realistic goals and objectives.

A goal is a general statement about what a system wishes to achieve. An objective is a concrete statement explaining how something will be achieved. Objectives, in other words, are how goals will be met. The consultant must help members of an organization develop goals and objectives that are achievable but must also be created within the limits of an organization's resources. The development of sound goals and objectives aimed at improving the functioning of a system takes a great deal of time and energy.

Stage Two: Scanning the System

Once the consultation process has begun, the practitioner must do a thorough assessment of the system. In small systems, this assessment can be accomplished in an informal fashion. Larger, more complex systems call for formal assessment strategies, including questionnaires, interviews, and other similar strategies. Blocher and Biggs (1983) conclude that this process is analogous to a practitioner doing a one-to-one interview with a single client; the major difference is that the client is a more complex system. Keeping this analogy in mind, once a thorough assessment has been conducted of an organization, the practitioner can begin an intervention strategy for changing the system.

Stage Three: Intervening

The choice of an intervention strategy is based on a carefully calculated approach. The approaches to consultation one can choose from include triadic and process. The kind of consultation demanded will be determined by the nature and complexity of the problem facing a given system. The assessment of the system conducted in stage two will determine the kind of consultation called for within an organization.

Stage Four: Enhancing Communication and Relationships

During this stage, the consultant concentrates on improving communication and building positive relationships within the organization. This process is best accomplished through active listening to members of the organization. It is critical to take a neutral position when members of the organization share feelings about how communication can be improved and relationships can be enhanced. This information needs to be built into the strategies for improving system functioning.

Stage Five: Fine-Tuning Objectives

The objectives identified in stage one must be fined-tuned to ensure that they can be implemented successfully. This process is accomplished with organizational input from all levels, including supervisors and direct service providers. If this kind of consensus cannot be achieved, organizational change will not be successful. The consultant also must ensure that the objectives after fine-tuning are realistic and that they can be achieved.

Stage Six: Introducing New Approaches

This stage is one of the most critical aspects of the consulting process. The actual behavioral changes that must occur if the goals and objectives are to be achieved are the focus of this stage. The consultant must have a good reading of the readiness of the organization to implement the planned changes. If the changes are implemented prematurely, the consulting process will be a failure. One strategy the consultant may wish to use is initially to implement easily achievable objectives and proceed with more complex ones later. This approach can be used to teach organizational members about the goal achievement process and help them gain confidence in bringing about organizational change.

Stage Seven: Maintaining New Behaviors

Once behavioral changes are made within an organization, these changes must be maintained. This process can be achieved by closely monitoring organization activity through various kinds of evaluation. It is important to seek input from all organizational members about improved strategies for maintaining and enhancing behaviors that improve organization functioning. In-service training can also be a useful tool for maintaining new behaviors critical to achieving organizational change. The kinds of in-service training needed should be determined by all organizational members, including supervisors and direct service providers.

Stage Eight: Evaluating the Consultation Process

This final stage involves the entire consultation process. The specific measures for the success of the consultation process are based on the degree to which the agreed-on goals and objectives for organizational change have been met. Since objectives are measurable and concrete, the success of the consultation process will be easy to determine.

TRAINING AS SOCIAL INTERVENTION

An ecological perspective suggests that problems experienced by individuals are based on their transactions with the larger social environment. As noted in Chapter 1, the ecological approach is seen as an answer to the narrow disease-oriented medical model. The notion that one's social environment plays a dominant role in determining one's social functioning replaces the traditional intrapsychic view for explaining individual behavior. An intrapsychic psychological orientation is based on the medical model, but such a view offers little for practitioners using an ecological approach because of its narrow explanation of human behavior.

An ecological perspective moves away from the "blaming the victim" position to a holistic approach, which argues that individual dysfunction is often the result of nonsupporting social systems that encompass the client's ecosystem. In traditional psychology, the labels used to describe clients (such as depressed, manicdepressive, and so on) are often a result of environmental conditions that do not provide the supports critical to a client's social functioning. Social skills training is a strategy that practitioners can use to help clients improve their capacity to cope with environmental pressures. This kind of training offers clients the basic skills critical for dealing effectively with obstacles in their environment. In a real sense, social skills training is a form of empowerment that helps clients manage and solve problems. McWhirter (1991) provides the following descriptive insight into the empowerment process resulting from social skills training:

Empowerment is the process by which people, organizations, or groups who are powerless (a) become aware of the power dynamics at work in their life context, (b) develop the skills and capacity for gaining some reasonable control over their lives, (c) exercise this control without infringing on the rights of others, and (d) support the empowerment of others in their community. (p. 224)

Empowerment helps clients exercise self-responsibility as well as experience an opportunity to change social structures that affect their lives. Such a strategy is the essence of an ecological approach to practice. The following social skills models presented by Carkhuff (1969) and Egan (1994) can be used as strategies that provide the tools to empower clients.

CARKHUFF'S SOCIAL SKILLS TRAINING MODEL

Carkhuff (1969) grounds his approach to social skills training in the work of Carl Rogers. Rogerian invention is client centered and is aimed at personal growth and development. Using the Rogerian philosophy, Carkhuff suggests that certain conditions are always present in the helping relationship. His model attempts to teach clients the behaviors and attributes of the helping relationship.

Carkhuff's model is also seen as an approach to training natural helpers in the community. Natural helpers can be very effective for empowering the community and changing the social structures that prevent individual growth and development. In other words, Carkhuff's model can be used not only as a strategy for improving social functioning of individual clients but also as a tool for empowering communities through a natural helper network.

The key components that the practitioner teaches clients through Carkhuff's model include the following:

1. Use of empathy and relationships
2. Respect for others
3. Definition presenting problems in a concrete manner
4. The importance of genuineness in relationships
5. Appropriate use of confrontation
6. The importance of immediacy.

Carkhuff's training approach uses specific techniques for teaching these skills. Once clients as well as natural helpers master these skills, they can become effective change agents not only in self-advocacy and empowerment but also as agents for empowering others.

EGAN'S SOCIAL SKILLS TRAINING MODEL

Egan (1994) offers a basic program presenting not only a theory of training social skills but also numerous experiential activities for helping individuals improve their interactional skills with others. Specifically, his training model attempts to teach the following kinds of social skills:

1. How to express directly what one is feeling
2. How to communicate clearly with others
3. How to listen to others objectively
4. How to be spontaneous and free in one's communication with others
5. How to respond to another's feelings in an appropriate fashion
6. How to live and communicate in the present
7. How to enjoy psychological closeness
8. How to communicate in a concrete fashion
9. How to strive for interdependence rather than dependence on others
10. How to be spontaneous and open in relationships.

Many of these social skills not only empower people to deal more effectively with their social environment but are seen as critical aspects of the emotionally healthy individual. Clearly, mastery of these skills will enhance one's ability to transact effectively with one's social environment.

CONCLUSION

Consultation and training are both useful activities that can enhance the practitioner's effectiveness. In a certain sense, both are strategies that can be used to improve the macrolevel functioning of large systems, including organizations and communities. In essence, consultation and training are ultimately tools that can enhance the ecological approach to practice.

The field of community psychology offers a highly developed literature on the use of consultation in practice. This chapter has attempted to translate this literature to the field of social work. The model offered in this chapter can be used for conducting consultation with systems of various sizes, particularly organizational systems. This chapter also discussed the levels at which one can involve the self in the consultation process: technical, collaborative, and facilitative. The nature of the problem confronting a system will determine the level at which one intervenes. It is not unusual to use all three levels during the consultation process, because they are not necessarily mutually exclusive and can thus be conducted jointly.

Training as an intervention strategy is important because it suggests that empowerment of clients is critical for social change. Training offers clients an approach that provides them with various tools to change their personal lives and to change whole systems, particularly the community system. The models of training offered in this chapter are those developed by Carkhuff (1969) and Egan (1994). The practitioner can use these approaches as effective training programs to bring about social change. In essence, training is a practice tool that can influence change at both the micro- and macrolevels of social intervention.

REFERENCES

Blocher, D. H., & Biggs, D. A. (1983). *Counseling psychology in community settings.* New York: Springer.

Carkhuff, R. R. (1969). *Helping and human relations: Vol. 1. Selection and training.* New York: Holt, Rinehart & Winston.

Egan, G. (1994). *The skilled helper: A problem-management approach to helping* (5th ed.). Pacific Grove, CA: Brooks/Cole.

McWhirter, E. H. (1991). Empowering in counseling. *Journal of Counseling and Development, 69,* 222–227.

Murphy, J. W., & Pardeck, J. T. (1991). *The computerization of human services agencies.* Westport, CT: Auburn House.

Chapter 6

Working with Organizations

Organizations are a dominant force in modern society. Most social workers conduct their professional practice within organizational settings. For practitioners to be effective, they must understand the classical theories that attempt to explain organizational life. In particular, they need to have insight into the formal and informal aspects of organizational behavior. Furthermore, the effective practitioner grounded in the ecological perspective must know how to improve organizational effectiveness. This chapter focuses on all of these critical issues.

TRADITIONAL ORGANIZATIONAL THEORY

Taylor (1911) and Weber (1947) are early organizational theorists who compared organizations to machines. Both theorists view social life as rational at the individual level as well as at the organizational level. Taylor's model of organization is based on scientific management; Weber's is grounded in the ideal-type bureaucratic model.

Scientific Management

Taylor (1911) has had a tremendous impact on modern organizations. Taylor argued that to maximize efficiency in an organizational setting, organizational behavior must be based on the time and motion needed to accomplish various tasks. Workers must be trained to perform simple tasks, and the completion of these tasks is viewed as the best strategy for maximizing efficiency and productivity. Taylor also had a low regard for workers; he concluded that workers do not have the capacity to be self-motivated. Consequently, tasks had to be simple so the worker could understand the relationship between the completion of a specific task followed by an external reward. When workers exceeded their minimum number of required tasks, they would be rewarded through a bonus system.

The limitations of scientific management are obvious. First, the activities required in many organizations simply cannot be broken down into simple tasks. Second, people are not like robots; they are complex beings motivated by complex reward systems. Third, scientific management does not fit the complexities of professional organizational life. Consequently, Taylor's model has little utility for understanding how modern organizations work and, specifically, it provides little insight into how people are motivated in the workplace.

The Bureaucratic Model

Weber's (1947) model of organization continues to have a great impact on how organizations are structured and viewed in modern society. Weber's bureaucratic model of organization is based on a machine model that must have certain components present to maximize efficiency and internal order. Specifically, the ideal-type organization has the following characteristics:

1. Impersonal social relationships
2. Appointment and promotion on the basis of merit
3. Specific authority obligations inherent to each organization position
4. A hierarchy of authority
5. Rules that cover behavior for performing specific tasks
6. Specification of positions.

Weber felt that it was critical for members of organizations not to relate to one another on a personal basis. His model of organizations concludes that impersonal social relationships prevent nepotism and ultimately create an organizational environment based on rational decision making. Weber argued that basing appointments on merit enhances organizational functioning. Furthermore, assigning authority to a position versus an individual is seen as a strategy for improving organizational efficiency. In essence, Weber felt that his ideal-type organization creates a social system that is rational and predictable in terms of organizational life.

As most people realize, there are many limitations to the Weberian model:

1. People do not behave like machines. Human behavior is extremely complex and often does not appear to be rational.

2. Rules cannot be created for every situation that occurs in the organizational setting. This phenomenon is particularly true of organizational settings composed of professionals. Furthermore, the human condition is too complex and variable to create a series of rules within an organizational setting to cover all possible situations.

3. Organizational activities, regardless of their efficiency, often take on a life of their own. This phenomenon is well known in the organizational setting. Selznick (1966) concludes that substructures within bureaucracies often place departmental interest over organization interest, and the result is inefficiency.

4. Informal groups exist in organizational settings. The bureaucratic model does not deal well with the informal structures of organizational life. Often informal leaders emerge out of this structure; these leaders have tremendous influence on organizational life.

5. Bureaucratic organizations appear to have high levels of efficiency; however, they have a low capacity for innovation. The lack of innovation in bureaucratic systems is a well-known problem. This situation is often intensified by the internal rules and regulations of the bureaucratic organization, which do not respond well to external changes.

6. The ability of individuals to make autonomous decisions is viewed as a negative behavior within bureaucratic structures. Individual autonomy is circumvented by creating red tape and paperwork that prevents individuals from disrupting the rational order created by the bureaucratic model.

Even though there are many positive aspects to bureaucratic organization, there are also numerous limitations, as just listed. Social workers are often confronted with various obstacles created by the bureaucratic structure, which prevent the effective delivery of services. Those practitioners grounded in an ecological approach to practice are well aware of the tremendous pressure bureaucratic systems place on the effective delivery of social services. The skilled practitioner working from an ecological perspective has the tools available to overcome many of the obstacles created by bureaucratic systems.

HUMAN-RELATIONS MODEL FOR ORGANIZATIONS

Weber's classical model has often been criticized for its lack of sensitivity to the human element within the organizational structure. McGregor (1960) responded to this situation by developing the human-relations model, an organizational structure that is supposed to integrate the human element into organizational life. McGregor argued that human beings will exercise self-direction and self-control in the workplace if they have a commitment to organizational goals. He suggested that persons typically have the capacity to offer a high degree of imagination and creativity to the solutions of organizational problems if they are allowed to do so. In essence, for many people work is not solely an activity that they do for only money but also for psychological satisfaction.

Etzioni (1964) summarizes the human-relations approach to work. These points significantly differ from Weber's bureaucratic position on work.

1. The amount of production a worker accomplishes is not a product of the worker's physical capacity but of his or her social capacity.

2. Psychological and noneconomic rewards play a central role in worker motivation and satisfaction.

3. Specialization within organizations creates isolation, and this is not an efficient or effective way to structure the division of labor within an organizational system.

4. Members of organizations react to organizational life as members of groups, not solely as individuals.

Etzioni's observations clearly suggest that complex organizations are far more than simple bureaucratic structures but instead are complex social systems that must meet the psychological needs of employees if they are to be effective.

At first glance, a human-relations model appears to include many important features often excluded from modern organizations. Even though there are many strengths to the human-relations approach, there are a number of limitations. One limitation is that not all organizations can be based on the human-relations model (e.g., the military, prisons, and other similar kinds of total institutions); however, few would argue that a human-relations approach is inappropriate for a mental health organization. Another limitation is that the model places too much emphasis on social factors, when other critical variables of organizational life must be considered for optimal organizational effectiveness and efficiency. A third limitation of the human-relations model is that it does not consider the importance of conflict as a process for promoting social change. Those grounded in the human-relations approach attempt to minimize conflict and to create harmony within the workplace. Conflict is critical to organizational development and change. Finally, even if the human-relations approach creates a pleasant work environment, it does not lessen the tediousness of tasks that must be accomplished in all organizational settings.

FORMAL AND INFORMAL ASPECTS OF ORGANIZATIONS

The formal aspects of complex organizations are often well articulated through rules and regulations. These formal aspects of organizations are critical to employees because they establish the ground rules for individual behavior; however, as noted by a number of organizational theorists (e.g., Davis, 1953; Dubin, 1962), the informal structure of organizational life is a powerful force that is critical to organizational effectiveness and efficiency.

One kind of informal organizational behavior often referred to as the grapevine is used to supplement or supplant the official channels of communication. This kind of behavior occurs over coffee breaks, in the lunchroom, and before or after meetings. The grapevine within the organization often allows employees to find out what is really occurring in the organization. Often the directives coming from the official channels of communication seem only to provide official validation for what is already known throughout the organization.

Informal behavior of organizations is an important source of change. Many organizations are resistant to change and innovation. New ideas and practices have a tendency to be seen as a threat to the status quo; the informal operation within any organizational system may be the only way that change will occur. In other words, the informal structure may be the only source of change and innovation within a rigid and sterile organizational system.

Informal organizational structure often has a tremendous influence over the opinions and attitudes of members. All complex organizations have unofficial leaders who are not a part of the official hierarchical structure but nonetheless have great influence over official leaders. Official leaders must listen closely to what the unofficial leaders are communicating to them. If the official hierarchical structure does not act appropriately on this information, the entire system can be paralyzed. Organizational change will only occur if the unofficial leaders agree with it.

AUTHORITARIAN AND LAISSEZ-FAIRE MANAGEMENT

Social service agencies often take on two extreme management approaches: authoritarian and laissez faire (Murphy & Pardeck, 1986). The authoritarian style of management is typically grounded in the bureaucratic tradition. It is based on the assumption that practitioners need extensive supervision and rules to ensure appropriate performance. The laissez-faire approach to management is grounded in the view that social workers need freedom and autonomy to deliver services effectively. Both views are based on misconception and indeed may stifle organization communication, inhibit worker personal growth, and generally contribute to a decline in job satisfaction.

The authoritarian and laissez-faire management styles view organizations in a hierarchical manner. Practitioners are seen as part of the organizational hierarchy and are expected to provide input through formalized structures. They are expected to achieve various goals and objectives in their work performance, but these are rarely clear because a lack of coordinated planning results in frustration and ineffective job performance.

Authoritarian organizations typically treat employees badly. Demands are often made with no accompanying explanation, and employees are treated as if their competence is being questioned. Obversely, laissez-faire management styles create structures in which workers wander aimlessly until administrators decide how and when a particular task should be completed. In both cases, joint worker–management planning is absent; thus authoritarian and laissez-faire management styles create ambiguity relative to how a specific job fits into the overall scheme of the larger organization. Since the authoritarian system was never designed to accommodate worker participation, it diminishes the worth of employee ideas; likewise, the laissez-faire management approach allows employees to work at their own pace and provides little or no supervision. Both of these management strategies create unnecessary frustration and stress for practitioners because the rationale that supports administrative decisions remains unknown (Murphy & Pardeck, 1986).

The authoritarian and laissez-faire styles of management both have a tendency to create irrelevant performance goals, if there are goals at all. In the authoritarian organization, supervisors impose what they feel are performance goals that are intrinsically related to the services performed by employees; in the absence of management, workers simply respond to whatever demands are placed on them from outside funding sources, such as state or federal governments. Both approaches create disorganization. In the former, practitioners must placate unreasonable demands from supervisors while attempting to delivery services; in the latter, workers are in constant fear of doing useless tasks because job demands are never defined clearly. Workers thus never reach a state of closure and ultimately lose interest in their work. For example, in the authoritarian system workers are rewarded for performing meaningless tasks. The absence of supervision in the laissez-faire organization leaves practitioners unclear about the quality and validity of their work.

Authoritarian and laissez-faire management approaches also have a serious impact on practitioners' creativity, which can lead to worker burnout. Under both approaches, practitioners spend a great deal of time investing energy in tasks that have no meaning and are unrelated to job performance. Management must provide meaningful feedback on a regular basis to ensure that workers are performing quality work. Both approaches are not designed to provide this kind of critical feedback, and thus they result in possible burnout and, at minimum, low morale.

MANAGEMENT STRATEGIES AND SUPPORTIVE WORK ENVIRONMENTS

Rensis Likert (1967, 1978) has designed an organizational structure that creates a work environment conducive to growth and development of workers. Likert's position suggests that organizations consist of ecosystems that enhance practitioner social functioning, which in turn leads to improved services for clients. Likert's approach, which he refers to as System 4, encourages both worker self-expression and the development of organizational and performance guidelines for directing and evaluating job performance.

Likert's System 4 is based on the idea that all program goals should be formulated by participative groups composed of supervisors and practitioners. Such an approach allows worker self-expression and management control. Likert's model of organization allows for the development of job-related skills, enhances peer support, clears communication channels, and improves workers' self-esteem (Murphy & Pardeck, 1986).

The management philosophy outlined in Likert's System 4 model negates many of the prevalent traditional managerial prejudices. Most of these are grounded in the bureaucratic approach to organization. Specifically, Likert (1) suggests that workers should be intimately involved in program planning; (2) views management systems as not oppressive by nature; and (3) states that a lack of planning is not the only method for encouraging individualism. These ideas should assist in reducing the problems resulting from an authoritarian system and the absence of management because both supervisors and workers are fully informed of the course of action the organization is taking (Murphy & Pardeck, 1986).

Likert's participative group approach to formulating organizational goals is based on a linking-pin approach to organizational structure. This style of management is one in which key personnel from each department participate in overlapping, cross-functional groups, thereby uniting a program because members are knowledgeable about a variety of subcomponents of an organization. Under this system, each department's work is the organization's work, because the structure that enhances in-group/out-group competition is eliminated. Likert's view of organization means that a program is fully integrated directly within the larger organization. This results in horizontal integration, not vertical, and in the following positive outcomes:

1. Higher productivity

2. Higher production goals

3. Better attitudes toward supervision

4. Less anxiety and frustration about job-related matters

5. Better overall work attitudes on the part of personnel.

These positive conditions are impossible to achieve under authoritarian and laissez-faire approaches to management, because such approaches lack meaningful participation in organizational goal setting by those who comprise the organization (Murphy & Pardeck, 1986).

Since social service agencies are increasing in sophistication and complexity, two major problems have emerged within human service systems. First, job alignment is critical—that is, individuals must be placed in the right position. Second, when programs expand, the growth is often overwhelming. Likert's linking-pin approach to organizational structure can alleviate pressures associated with these two problem areas (Murphy & Pardeck, 1986).

Under the first condition, if workers are not placed in the correct position, they often become frustrated and may experience burnout. This situation is not necessarily the result of workers' being unable to adjust to work requirements in social service programs but results from improper job demands created by the growing complexity of an organization. Specifically, when an organization becomes more complex because of changing job demands, managers must have the skill to analyze if the job can still be performed adequately by a worker (Murphy & Pardeck, 1986).

Second, when an organization expands there is a tendency for workers to feel overwhelmed. Supervisors must help workers deal with the mystique associated with organizations when they attain a high degree of sophistication and complexity. It is critical for supervisors to transmit information to workers that helps them understand the changes occurring within the organization. Workers must not feel isolated from the organization, particularly during times of rapid change (Murphy & Pardeck, 1986).

When new technologies such as computers are introduced to the workplace, workers often feel frustration and, in general, organizational turmoil is common. In human service agencies, computer technology is often introduced to help practitioners improve data collection on clients, conduct research, and make diagnoses. If practitioners do not have input into how these new technologies should be used, and if they are not trained in how to use them, they become frustrated and morale will drop within the organization. According to Murphy and Pardeck (1986), authoritarian and laissez-faire management styles often treat innovation as a test for workers and usually take a wait-and-see attitude until the change is complete. The Likert approach uses a much different orientation to change; specifically, a climate is created that both facilitates the diffusion of knowledge throughout the organization and provides an atmosphere conducive for nontraumatic learning. Likert argues that social change must not simply occur but should be managed (cited in Murphy & Pardeck, 1986).

Likert's linking-pin approach to management fosters work environments that enhance organizational change. It supports relationships that Likert believes are important to advancing organizational goals and objectives. This is accomplished by ensuring that organizations are not simply connected by one-directional communication channels but are functionally linked to each other. This system creates extensive networks throughout the organization that enhance group cohesion and supportive relationships among staff members (Murphy & Pardeck, 1986).

Unlike the bureaucratic approach to organizations, the Likert approach suggests that information should not simply trickle down through organizational channels but should be shared directly by both administrators and workers. This approach improves both the quality and quantity of information available to workers. Change is also less traumatic because persons receive reliable information. Furthermore, training is viewed in a more favorable light because it is relevant to the new jobs that must be done. Within the human service organization, a linking-pin structure unites administrators and practitioners because they understand each other and share information. Both feel that they are participating in the development of organizational goals and that they have meaningful input into how the larger organization works.

The linking-pin approach also allows workers to experience self-actualization because they are allowed to be creative and have a sense of control over what happens in the workplace. Worker creativity is important to self-actualization, and Likert's approach to organizational structure encourages this kind of behavior by ensuring that workers have meaningful input into the organizational decision-making process. Furthermore, the Likert approach to organizations encourages job rotation; this strategy results in workers expanding their competence by learning new jobs within other areas of the organization. This approach accomplishes two aims: (1) Workers are moved out of a routine that may stifle initiative, and (2) work appraisals are made to ensure that a person is placed in the proper position. The linking-pin structure allows the flexibility critical to job enrichment and rotation (Murphy & Pardeck, 1986).

CONCLUSION

This chapter argues that the traditional approaches to organizational structures are dated and do not enhance productivity of workers. Unfortunately, many social service agencies are based on traditional organizational approaches, even though these structures cause poor service delivery. Likert's System 4 management approach is an alternative to traditional organizational systems.

Likert's approach to organizational structure recognizes the importance of the various ecosystems that comprise the larger environment people work in. Specifically, Likert argues that systems must be horizontal, not vertical, to enhance worker input. This kind of collaboration between workers and supervisors is clearly a strategy grounded in the ecological approach to social work practice. The sharing of information between workers and supervisors helps democratize complex organizational systems. As noted earlier, democratization is a core principle of an ecological approach to social work practice. Finally, the Likert approach to organizational development suggests that ecosystems within the workplace must encourage creativity and initiative of workers. Such an orientation is clearly aligned with an ecological approach to social work practice.

REFERENCES

Davis, K. (1953). Management communication and the grapevine. *Harvard Business Review, 14*, 44–49.

Dubin, R. (1962). Power, function, and organization. *Pacific Sociological Review, 6,* 16–24.

Etzioni, A. (1964). *Complex organizations.* New York: Holt, Rinehart & Winston.

Likert, R. (1967). *The human organization.* New York: McGraw-Hill.

———. (1978). An improvement cycle for human resource development. *Training and Development Journal, 16,* 16–18.

McGregor, D. (1960). *The human side of enterprise.* New York: McGraw-Hill.

Murphy, J. W., & Pardeck, J. T. (1986). The "burnout syndrome" and management style. *The Clinical Supervisor, 4,* 35–44.

Selznick, P. (1966). *TVA and grass roots: A study in the sociology of formal organizations.* Berkeley: University of California Press.

Taylor, F. W. (1911). *The principles of scientific management.* New York: Harper & Row.

Weber, M. (1947). *The theory of social and economic organization.* New York: Oxford University Press.

Chapter 7

Social Work Assessment

Assessment is often associated with the term *diagnosis*. Social workers grounded in the ecological approach will find the term *assessment* a more appealing concept for understanding a presenting problem because it involves holistic analysis, whereas diagnosis is a narrow concept grounded in the medical model.

When the practitioner does an assessment of a client's situation, he or she uses a holistic approach involving factors related not only to the individual but also to the individual's social environment. In essence, assessment involves an analysis of the client's micro- and macrolevel environments.

Max Siporin (1975, p. 219) defines assessment as "a process and a product of understanding on which action is based. That is, it is the collection and analysis of information." This information, in turn, guides the intervention process. Johnson (1995) adds to the definition by suggesting that assessment is a complex process that has a number of important characteristics:

1. Assessment is an ongoing process between the client and practitioner. As the practitioner works with the client, new information continues to emerge throughout the helping process that increases insight into the transaction of the client with his or her environment.

2. Assessment is a twofold process, focusing both on understanding the client's presenting problem and developing a plan of intervention to solve the problem.

3. Assessment is a process based on mutuality between client and practitioner. The client is engaged in all aspects of the assessment process.

4. The assessment process is holistic. It involves the generation of information from all parts of the social environment as well as data on the client.

5. Assessment identifies needs in life situations, defines presenting problems, and attempts to explain the origin of problems.

6. Assessment is an individualized process based on the premise that no two situations are alike. Assessment considers the different parts of the situation and views the parts in a holistic fashion.

7. No assessment is ever complete because of the limits of human understanding of complex problems. There will always be unknowns associated with the assessment process because of human limitations.

8. When conducting the assessment process, the practitioner must view problems horizontally and vertically. In the early stages, horizontal assessment is most helpful. That is, the situation is examined in breadth to identify all possible parts, interactions, and relationships. As the assessment process proceeds, the situation is examined vertically; that is, it is examined in greater depth.

What should be clear concerning the assessment process as developed by Johnson (1995) is the holistic and ongoing nature of the process. However, a major limitation of the process is the subjective judgments practitioners must make about client functioning based on incomplete information. These subjective judgments can be more accurate if the practitioner uses valid and reliable measurement tools.

MEASURING PROBLEMS

Numerous technologies are available that help practitioners make more accurate assessments in the treatment process. Accuracy, or validity of an assessment, rests on the quality of measurement performed by the practitioner. Measurement as a process is defined as describing abstract concepts in terms of specific indicators by the assignment of numbers or other symbols to these indicants in accordance with rules (Corcoran & Fischer, 1994, p. 11).

In the social sciences, there are two strategies for conducting measurement: quantitative and qualitative.

Quantitative measurement means the placement of phenomena into specific categories created prior to investigation and the assignment of numbers to these categories. This process allows the practitioner to quantify information and then to conduct statistical analysis. Data are normally collected through the use of questionnaires, structured observation, and interviews. The reduction of phenomena to numbers means that computer technology can be used in all aspects of the assessment process and ultimately in treatment intervention.

Qualitative measurements involve nonnumerical explorations of phenomena. Narrative techniques are often used in qualitative assessment. Qualitative data collection is unstructured in the form of interviewing, observation, and logs and journals. The tradition within the field of social work is to stress qualitative measurement over quantitative measurement. Thus the interview has emerged as the central focus for assessing presenting problems of clients.

TYPES OF MEASUREMENT

Practitioners often argue that many client problems are unmeasureable. This is based on the assumption that what practitioners treat in practice is often so complex and abstract that certain phenomena cannot be grounded in the world of measurement. Practitioners argue that certain phenomena can only be understood through impression. If one grounds oneself in solid theory and social science, there is little basis for this position. The following techniques can be used for measuring most phenomena critical to accurate assessment of presenting problems of clients.

Behavioral Observation

Behavioral observation is based on the actual observing of a client's functioning (Corcoran & Fischer, 1994). This might be overt behavior, such as kissing and walking, or covert behavior, such as thinking and feeling.

There are three basic approaches for measuring or counting behavior (Corcoran & Fischer, 1994). One approach is the frequency of the behavior. Simply put, how often does it occur? A second strategy is the duration of the behavior—that is, how long it lasts. A third approach is the interval between behaviors. Some behaviors occur so often and for so long that it is not useful to use frequency or duration recording. What must be done as an alternative is to record the observations at various intervals. The practitioner implements this approach by observing behavior over a period of time and then dividing this period into equal blocks of time. This strategy allows the practitioner to observe if the behavior increases or decreases during the different blocks of time being observed.

Observation of the client in his or her natural environment yields invaluable data because it allows the practitioner to gain insight into the person-in-the-environment transaction. The assessment and treatment of the transactional process of the client with his or her environment is central to practitioners grounded in the ecological approach.

Self-Anchored and Rating Scales

This is an all-measurement procedure that allows the practitioner and the client to construct an instrument to measure client functioning (Bloom, 1975). The initial step in the instrument's construction is to focus on the intensity of a problem as perceived by the client. Once this information is identified, the practitioner asks the client to identify feelings associated with the problem when it is most severe. This information is viewed as one end of the scale. Likewise, the client is requested to note feelings when the problem is not present.

Each extreme of the self-anchored scale is translated into numbers. For example, when a problem is present, the numbers on the scale might be 1 to 2, with 3 being a neutral zone of feeling. When a problem is absent, positive feelings may range from 4 to 5 on the scale. The result is a scale ranging from 1 to 5, and this scale allows the client to translate feelings into numbers.

A rating scale is similar to the self-anchored scale; however, the major difference is that the client does not rate himself or herself—someone else does. This other person is often the practitioner (Corcoran & Fischer, 1994).

Client Logs

Client logs are journals kept by the person receiving services. They are more or less formal records of events that occur in the client's life. Logs are useful because the client can write down information as it occurs. This allows more precise understanding of the presenting problem versus recollection of the information after it has occurred.

Corcoran and Fischer (1994) identify two purposes of client logs: (1) They allow a more accurate assessment because important information can be pinpointed, and (2) they provide an ongoing record of a client's progress throughout the treatment process. This record allows the client and practitioner to gain an understanding of the effectiveness of the intervention process.

Unobtrusive Measures

These are measures that the client is not aware of when assessment is being conducted. There are two forms of unobtrusive measures. One is archival data that are kept for other purposes but can be used as a tool to judge treatment effectiveness. The second is behavioral products data, such as the number of cigarette butts left in an ashtray after an assessment interview is conducted. These kinds of data suggest the anxiety state of the client during the interview as measured by the number of cigarettes smoked. Examples of unobtrusive measures for a client who is a student include grades earned and attendance rates at school.

Standardized Measures

Within the field of social work and related disciplines, numerous standardized clinical instruments have been developed. Standardized measures are those that have uniform procedures for administration and scoring and contain a series of structured questions or statements designed to elicit information from the client (Corcoran & Fischer, 1994). Many standardized measures have been computerized.

Since so many standardized measures are now available, Corcoran and Fischer (1994) have outlined two important criteria that can be used to help the practitioner identify those most useful for practice. First, the standardized measures must have uniform items, scoring procedures, and methods of administration. Second, quality standardized measures will have certain types of information available. Specifically, they will include data on their reliability, validity, scoring, administration, and norms. Without these kinds of data, the practitioner cannot make an informed judgment about the measure's scientific soundness.

Hudson's (1988) Clinical Assessment System (CAS) is one of the most extensive standardized measurement packages now available to practitioners. The CAS is a compilation of all Hudson's scales, each based on the single-subject format. The CAS includes scales for measuring depression, self-esteem, marital discord, sexual discord, parent–child relationships, intrafamilial stress, and peer relationships. The CAS system is also computerized.

PRINCIPLES OF MEASUREMENT

Measurement of a client's problem is an intricate part of quality assessment. If the practitioner's aim is to assess a presenting problem accurately, he or she must have tools available that measure phenomena accurately. Corcoran and Fischer (1994) offer a number of principles that can assist the practitioner in identifying useful measurement tools.

Utility

Utility refers to how practical a measurement tool is for practice. An instrument that allows one to improve services and provides accurate feedback has obvious utility. Instruments that are short, are easy to score and interpret, and tap clinically relevant problems have the greatest utility for practice.

Suitability and Acceptability

To meet the principle of suitability and acceptability, an instrument must be aimed at the appropriate intellectual and emotional level of the client. Instruments that require sophisticated vocabulary or reading levels often are not suitable or acceptable for practice.

Instruments that are suitable and acceptable for assessment and intervention should measure the client's problem accurately. The client must also feel that the instruments are useful and must be willing to use them during treatment. If the client does not feel that the instrument will help him or her solve a presenting problem, the instrument will not be helpful to the assessment or treatment process.

Sensitivity

Useful measurements for practice must be sensitive to changes that occur in the client's life, even if these changes are modest. If an instrument is not sensitive to this kind of change, the client's progress may go undetected. Given the principle of sensitivity, only those instruments that are scientifically sound will be useful to the assessment process. Specifically, they must be reliable and valid.

Directness

Directness refers to how the score generated from the instrument reflects actual behavior, feelings, and thoughts. Instruments that assess overt behavior are direct measures; however, indirect measures that are symbols of problems are also available to practitioners, such as the Thematic Apperception Test (TAT). Often instruments fall somewhere between direct and indirect measures. However, instruments that measure direct behavior are most useful to practice. Indirect measures have numerous problems in the area of validity. They also have limitations for helping the practitioner assess the magnitude or intensity of a client's problem.

COMPUTER TECHNOLOGY

The role of computer technology has greatly expanded in social work practice in the 1990s. Computer technology is viewed as useful in treatment because it performs tasks inexpensively and efficiently and is theoretically unaffected by personal biases (Pardeck & Murphy, 1990).

The computer can be a useful tool in an ecological approach to practice because it allows one to conduct large-scale assessment and to follow the success of treatment in a precise manner. Computer technology is now available that helps practitioners identify symptoms and render clinical assessments. Recent developments by Mattaini (1993) in the area of computer technology offer practitioners tools for doing computerized assessment and intervention grounded in ecological theory. This new technology offers the practitioner the following assessment tools: ecomaps, sequential ecomaps, contingency diagrams, concurrent graphing, and the computerized Visual EcoScan.

However, the use of computer technology has not gone unchallenged. Numerous questions have been raised about the dehumanizing effects of this technology, including the negative impact it may have on the therapeutic process. Pardeck and Murphy (1990) have argued that if practitioners are well aware of the potential ethical issues surrounding the use of computer technology in practice and its limitations, this kind of technology can enhance social work practice.

Computerized Testing and Inventories

Computerized assessment has been in development since the early 1950s. In the 1990s, there has been a proliferation of new developments in the area of computerized assessment. Computerized assessment is particularly useful to practice because it provides the benefits of standardized paper and pencil instruments in computerized format. This format allows the practitioner to generate instrument scores quickly, accurately, and efficiently. Many computerized inventories are easy to use and are relatively inexpensive.

In the 1990s, the computerized assessment instruments that appear to have the most promise are those that use a branching approach to assessment. An illustration is computer-based instruments that assess the potential for suicide. Such an instrument asks the client questions about previous suicide attempts; if questions do not apply to the client, the program skips over those items and thus branches off into other areas of inquiry. This kind of accurate case history reporting allows for more valid predictions about the client's future behavior. Computer-based instruments based on branching are available for numerous clinical problems.

Wodarski (1990) has developed an extensive list of inventories now available for use on the personal computer. These instruments continue to be created at a rapid rate. Examples of inventories now available for practice include the following:

- Adjective Checklist
- Bender Visual Motor Gestalt Test
- Career Assessment Inventory
- Clinical Analysis Questionnaire
- Million Adolescent Personality Inventory
- Minnesota Multiphasic Personality Inventory (MMPI)
- Multidimensional Personality Questionnaire
- Self-Description Inventory
- Strong-Campbell Interest Inventory
- Word and Number Assessment Inventory.

New developments continue in the area of computerized assessment. Such technology can be useful if the practitioner realizes the strengths and limitations of the technology.

Expert Systems and Social Intervention

More sophisticated computerized programs are now available that go well beyond computerized assessment. These include those that attempt to duplicate the decision-making process by an expert in a given field who is theoretically devoid of capriciousness. An expert system is based on the protocol used by decision makers to find solutions to problems. The process used by an expert to a solve problem is built into a software package. Expert systems are available in the areas of medicine, psychology, social work, and psychiatry.

An example of an expert system is the Diagnostic Interview Schedule (DIS), which is used to identify psychiatric disorders (Comings, 1984). Information about a problem is obtained from a flow-chart methodology. The following example is a probe routine used to determine whether a yes answer means that symptoms (Sx) are caused by drugs, alcohol, or an incident such as a head injury (Pardeck & Murphy, 1990, p. 80):

Question: "Have you ever had prolonged periods when you felt depressed?"

NO: (routine ends)

YES: (Go to next question[s])

Question: "Did you tell any other professional about (Sx)?"

Question: "Did you take medication for (Sx) more than once?"

Question: "Did (Sx) interfere with your life or activities a lot?"

ALL NO: (This means sympтons are not due to psychiatric problem)

FIRST YES: (Ask following questions)

Question: "Was (Sx) the result of a physical illness or injury?"

YES: (Go to A in box D)

NO: (Go to No. 3)

Question: "Was (Sx) always the result of a physical illness or injury (such as . . .)?

Yes: Record all

NO: (proceed)

Through this procedure for charting responses that probe questions, rational decision making is enhanced. There is obviously a great deal of controversy over the use of expert systems in practice. However, if the practitioner understands their limitations, he or she might find them useful to support the assessment and treatment process grounded in the ecological approach.

ECOLOGICAL ASSESSMENT

Chapter 1 presented three major concepts critical to the ecological assessment process: transaction, behavioral setting, and ecosystem. This section elaborates on the use of these concepts in the assessment process.

Transactional Assessment

Transaction is a complex process and thus causes difficulty for those who attempt to assess it. Johnson (1995) argues that there are guides and tools available for conducting transactional assessment. Given this state, practitioners must also rely heavily on their creativity and ability to understand and make sense of complex situations. They should also use the assessment approaches offered earlier in this chapter, which can assist them in conducting more valid transactional assessment. These approaches include, but are not limited to, behavioral observation, client logs, and standardized measures.

When conducting transactional assessment, the practitioner's major focus is on how the client interacts with his or her environment. The concept of transaction suggests that a reciprocal process exists between the client and environment and that each shapes the other. The environment contributes to the client's adjustment, the client's behaviors create unique responses with the environment, and both affect each other.

To conduct an accurate transactional assessment, the practitioner must assess the functioning of a number of key systems in the client's life, including individuals, families, organizations, and the larger community. As stressed in this book, effective practice must include all of these systems not only in the assessment process but also in the treatment that follows.

Behavioral observation is a useful assessment approach that provides insight into the transactional process. By observing overt behaviors, the practitioner can assess the actual interaction of the client with his or her family system or other relevant systems in the client's social environment. Through the observational process, the practitioner gains insight into how the client affects other systems and how the systems influence the client. For example, if a client is viewed as disturbed by individuals who encompass the various systems in the client's environment, these systems will probably trigger disturbed responses from the client. The practitioner can use observational techniques to assess thoroughly how the client and various systems in the client's environment trigger disturbed responses. The goal of treatment, with disturbing behavior being the presenting problem, would be to help the client and the social system related to the client alter the transactional process in such a manner that the disturbed behaviors are eliminated.

Client logs have obvious utility for assessing the transactional process. The client log can be used as a tool to record the actual events occurring before and after problem situations in the client's life. The client log is thus a record that the client can use to gain insight into problematic transactions with his or her environment. A goal of treatment would be to alter the client's environment in such a way that he or she could avoid those situations that cause problems.

Standardized measures are highly useful for assessing the transactional process because they are designed to provide valid assessment on an ongoing basis. The practitioner can use standardized measures to develop baseline information over a given time period that will result in valid transactional assessment. Chapter 8 covers standardized measurement instruments.

Behavioral Setting

The behavioral setting as an approach to ecological assessment was developed by Barker (1968). Behavioral settings (Blocher & Biggs, 1983) are natural phenomena that have a self-generated space–time locus occurring within the social environment. Behavioral settings have two components: (1) behavior and (2) nonpsychological objects that transact with behavior. Behavioral settings are stable and have a major impact on the behavior occurring in them. Barker (1968), for example, reports the impact that large and small schools have on students. He concludes that students in small schools compared to those in large schools reported having greater life satisfaction, greater challenges, and a greater feeling of being valued.

Blocher and Biggs (1983) view the behavioral setting as a unit in the ecological environment. Aspects of a behavioral setting include (1) nonbehavioral factors such as time, space, and objects; (2) standing behavioral patterns such as patterns of interaction in the workplace; and (3) relationships between behavioral and nonbehavioral factors. Thorough ecological assessment will include this kind of information. What is important about the behavioral setting is its influence on individual functioning. A key strategy for intervention is to improve and change a behavioral setting with the goal of enhancing the social functioning of individuals.

Ecosystems

Ecosystem assessment involves analysis of the conglomeration of various ecologies in the client's environment, including the self, family, and larger community. Each of the person's ecosystems has a dynamic impact on the person's social well-being.

The ecosystem is not necessarily a novel concept to the field of social work; however, it is a powerful concept that suggests that the client cannot be juxtaposed with the environment but instead is an inextricable part of it. The client's ecosystem is made up of the various subsystems in the client's life and must be an intricate part of the assessment process.

A client's social functioning is seen as a result of a client's transactions with the ecosystem that comprises the client's environment. The concept of ecosystem shifts the focus of understanding from the individual's personality and behavioral functioning to the transactions that exist between the individual and his or her ecosystem.

Important tools that can help the practitioner assess the client's ecosystem include the EcoScan and the Social Support Network Analysis (Johnson, 1995). The EcoScan is a tool that provides a pictorial representation of the relationships that exist in the client's environment. These relationships include the various subsystems—family, school, and so forth—that comprise the client's ecosystem. The EcoScan makes identification of problematic transactional processes more apparent. The Social Support Network Analysis (Johnson, 1995) focuses on the significant support resources in the client's ecosystem. It allows for identification of natural supports in the client's social environment and should thus be used as a complement to the EcoScan assessment. Mattaini's (1993) computerized program, which creates a Visual EcoScan and Social Support Network information, is a practical way to use the aforementioned assessment approaches. Not only does the Visual EcoScan provide information on the client's ecosystem, but it also offers useful information about the transactional process between the client and the various subsystems in the client's ecosystem.

CONCLUSION

Assessment is the process of developing a detailed analysis of the client's environment. The quality of assessment is based on the preciseness of the measurements used to assess the client's ecosystem. This chapter offers not only the principles of sound social measurement but also the tools that can be used to measure presenting problems.

Computer technology has emerged as a tool that can be used effectively in the ecological assessment process. Computers offer not only computerized testing and inventories but also expert systems programs, which can enhance the assessment process. Even though practitioners can conduct ecological assessment without the use of computer technology, mastery of computer technology will facilitate the efficiency and effectiveness of the assessment process. If the practitioner uses computer technology in practice, he or she must be well aware of its limitations and the potential dehumanizing effect of computers on social service delivery. The effective practitioner using computer technology in practice must clearly understand the ethical issues related to this technology.

Finally, this chapter elaborates on the core concepts critical to ecological assessment: transaction, behavioral setting, and ecosystem. It reviewed a number of measurement strategies that can enhance the validity of the assessment process.

REFERENCES

Barker, R. (1968). *Ecological psychology. Stanford, CA: Stanford University Press.*

Blocher, D. H., & Biggs, D. A. (1983). *Counseling psychology in community settings.* New York: Springer.

Bloom, M. (1975). *The paradox of helping: Introduction to the philosophy of scientific practice.* New York: Wiley.

Comings, D. E. (1984). A computerized diagnostic interview schedule (DIS) for psychiatric disorder. In M. D. Schwartz (Ed.), *Using computers in clinical practice* (pp. 195–203). New York: Haworth Press.

Corcoran, K., & Fischer, J. (1994). *Measures for clinical practice* (2nd ed.). New York: The Free Press.

Hudson, W. (1988). *CAS: The clinical assessment system.* Tallahassee, FL: WALMYR.

Johnson, L. (1995). *Social work practice: A generalist approach* (5th ed.). Needham Heights, MA: Allyn & Bacon.

Mattaini, M. (1993). *Visual EcoScan for clinical practice.* Washington, DC: NASW Press.

Pardeck, J. T., & Murphy, J. W. (Eds.). (1990). *Computers in human services: An overview for clinical and welfare services.* New York: Harwood Academic.

Siporin, M. (1975). *Introduction to social work practice.* New York: Macmillan.

Wodarski, J. S. (1990). Practical computer applications in the psychotherapy process. In J. T. Pardeck & J. W. Murphy (Eds.), *Computers in human services: An overview for clinical and welfare services* (pp. 21–34). New York: Harwood Academic.

Chapter 8

Instruments for Ecological Assessment and Intervention

Accurate assessment is a necessity for effective social work practice (Wodarski, 1981). Numerous assessment instruments are available that involve little time, energy, or cost to administer. These assessment tools are designed to measure various components critical to conducting an ecological analysis of a client's presenting problem. These instruments are designed to conduct assessment at the individual, family, and environmental levels. Many of the instruments are also available in computer format, which increases their ease of use in social work practice. The goal of this chapter is to review a variety of assessment instruments that will facilitate assessment and treatment from an ecological perspective.

The instruments discussed in this chapter include behavior rating scales, self-report inventories, structured interviews, and observational coding systems. Behavior rating scales are completed by an informed source in reference to the behavioral characteristics of another person, whereas the traditional questionnaire is an example of the self-report inventory. Behavior rating scales and self-report inventories are user friendly and easier to administer than the structured interview or direct observation. They also provide objective information about the success of treatment intervention.

The structured interview, which consists of standardized questions and responses, can provide extensive information on a client's social functioning and give the practitioner an opportunity to clarify questions and problems for more detailed information. Observational coding systems involve observing and recording the frequency of certain behaviors in a naturalistic or structured social situation. This approach obviously involves a great deal of time and effort on the part of the practitioner.

USING AND SELECTING ASSESSMENT INSTRUMENTS

The most critical factor in selecting an assessment instrument is its reliability and validity. The instruments reviewed in this chapter have acceptable reliability and validity. This means that they consistently measure the phenomena being assessed at the same levels and do so accurately.

The practitioner must become familiar with the assessment instruments reviewed in this chapter prior to their use. This chapter provides the reference source for the assessment instrument as well as information on the administration, scoring, and interpretation of the instruments.

When the practitioner uses assessment instruments, the client must provide informed consent. The client should also be told what the assessment instrument attempts to measure and who will see the information generated from the instrument. If the practitioner keeps these important points in mind, the instruments can be used as effective treatment tools.

ECOLOGICAL ASSESSMENT

Research suggests that social functioning is heavily influenced by complex problems occurring in one's ecosystem. The ecological approach offers a variety of strategies for assessing the client's functioning at multiple levels: individual, family, and environmental (Humphreys & Ciminero, 1979). The assessment instruments reviewed assess individual, child, and parent functioning (individual level); family interaction (family level); and environment (ecosystem level).

Individual Level

The following instruments are available for conducting assessment at the individual level. These assessment instruments are aimed at assessing individual social functioning and child and parent social functioning.

Adolescent Alcohol Involvement Scale (Mayer & Filstead, 1979). This fourteen-item self-report inventory categorizes adolescent alcohol use and abuse along a continuum from abstinence to misuse. This instrument demonstrated high test–retest reliability in screening adolescent populations for alcohol misuse. It is available from the Department of Psychiatry and Behavioral Sciences, Northwestern University, Chicago, IL 60611.

Adult–Adolescent Parenting Inventory (Bavolek, 1984). This thirty-two-item self-report inventory measures parenting strengths and weaknesses in four areas: inappropriate developmental expectations, lack of empathy toward children's needs, belief in the use of corporal punishment, and reversal of parent–child roles. Adult or adolescent parents or prospective parents respond to each item on a five-point scale (from "strongly agree" to "strongly disagree"). This instrument is available from Family Development Resources, Inc., 767 Second Avenue, Eau Claire, WI 54703.

Beck Depression Inventory (Beck, 1967). This twenty-one-item self-report inventory is one of the most widely used measures of depression in clinical practice. Respondents indicate on a scale from zero to three the severity of their current symptoms. This test is available from The Psychological Corporation, 555 Academic Court, San Antonio, TX 78204.

Behavior Problem Checklist (Quay, 1977). This fifty-five-item behavior-rating scale measures the types and degree of behavior problems in children and adolescents. A parent or teacher completes the three-point scale. Four subscales identify conduct problems, personality problems, inadequacy–immaturity, and socialized delinquency. This instrument is available from Donald R. Peterson, School of Professional Psychology, Busch Campus, Rutgers University, New Brunswick, NJ 08903.

Child Behavior Checklist (Achenbach & Edelbrock, 1979). This 118-item behavior-rating scale is one of the most widely used measures of children's problem behaviors. There are parallel forms for parents and teachers to complete about children ages four to sixteen. Respondents rate a variety of behaviors on a three-point scale. The checklist measures internalizing syndromes (i.e., depression, immaturity) and externalizing syndromes (i.e., aggression, hyperactivity). This checklist is available from Dr. Maria Kovacs, Western Psychiatric Institute and Clinic, 201 Desoto Street, Pittsburgh, PA 15213.

Child's Attitude toward Father and Mother Scales (Hudson, 1982). These separate twenty-five-item self-report inventories, rated on a one-to-five continuum, measure the extent, degree, or severity of problems a child age twelve or older has with his or her father or mother. This test is available from Richard D. Irwin, 181 Ridge Road, Homewood, IL 60473.

Children's Beliefs about Parental Divorce Scale (CBAPDS) (Kurdek & Berg, 1987). This thirty-six-item instrument is designed to measure children's beliefs about their parents' divorce. The instrument uses a yes/no format for responses to statements. Designed for children ages eight to fourteen, this is one of the few scales that measures children's beliefs about divorce. It is available from Larry Kurdek, Wright State University, Dayton, OH 45435.

Children's Depression Inventory (Kovacs, 1981). This twenty-seven-item self-report inventory, a modified version of the Beck Depression Inventory, measures overt symptoms of childhood depression, including sadness, suicidal ideation, and sleep and appetite disturbances. Children ages eight to fourteen respond on a three-point scale to the items. This test is available from Dr. Maria Kovacs, Western Psychiatric Institute and Clinic, 201 Desoto Street, Pittsburgh, PA 15213.

Children's Cognitive Assessment Questionnaire (CCAQ) (Zatz & Chassing, 1983). This forty-item instrument measures self-defeating and self-enhancing cognition associated with test anxiety and is useful for practitioners working in school or residential settings. The instrument uses a true/false format for responses to items and is designed for children ages nine to twelve. It is available from the authors of an article entitled "Cognitions of Anxious Children" in the *Journal of Consulting and Clinical Psychology, 51,* 526–534.

Children's Perceived Self-Control (CPSC) Scale (Humphreys, 1982). This eleven-item instrument measures self-control from a cognitive-behavioral perspective and is designed for children eight to twelve years of age. The instrument addresses interpersonal self-control, personal self-control, and self-evaluation and uses a "usually yes" or "usually no" format for responses to statements. It is available from Laura Humphrey, Ph.D., Department of Psychology, Northwestern University Medical School, 320 E. Huron, Chicago, IL 60611.

Depression Self-Rating Scale (DSRS) (Birleson, 1981). This instrument measures the extent and severity of depression in children. It uses eighteen items to measure depression in children between the ages of seven and thirteen. The scale includes items on a three-point scale that measures mood, physiological and somatic complaints, and cognitive aspects of depression. It is available from the authors of an article entitled "The Validity of Depression Disorders in Childhood and the Development of a Self-Rating Scale: A Research Report," *Journal of Child Psychology and Psychiatry, 22*, 73–88.

Developmental Profile II (Alpern, Boll, & Shearer, 1980). This 186-item behavior-rating scale measures the functioning of children from birth to age nine in five areas: physical, self-help, social, academic, and communication. The age-graded items are rated either pass or fail. The instrument can be completed in 20 to 40 minutes by a service provider employing knowledge of the child's skills, observations, and/or parent interviews. It is available from Psychological Development Publications, PO Box 3198, Aspen, CO 81611.

Generalized Contentment Scale (Hudson, 1982). This twenty-five-item self-report inventory, rated in a one-to-five continuum, measures the degree, severity, or magnitude of nonpsychotic depression and focuses largely on affective aspects of depression. It is available from Richard D. Irwin, 181 Ridge Road, Homewood, IL 60473.

Implicit Parental Learning Theory Interview (IPLET) (Honig, Caldwell, & Tannenbaum, 1973). This forty-five-item, 45-minute structured interview (twenty items for IPLETs 5 and 6) is designed to inventory the techniques a parent uses to deal with developmentally appropriate behaviors of preschool children. Five separate forms are available for use with parents of children ages one to four and five to six. This interview is available from Family Development Research Program, Syracuse University, College for Human Development, 206 Slocum Hall, Syracuse, NY 13244.

Index of Self-Esteem (Hudson, 1982). This twenty-five-item self-report inventory, rated on a one-to-five continuum, measures the degree, severity, or magnitude of a client's problem with self-esteem. It is available from Richard D. Irwin, 181 Ridge Road, Homewood, IL 60473.

Index of Parental Attitudes (Hudson, 1982). This twenty-five-item self-report inventory, rated on a one-to-five continuum, measures the extent, severity, or magnitude of parent–child relationship problems as perceived and reported by the parent in reference to a child of any age. It is available from Richard D. Irwin, 181 Ridge Road, Homewood, IL 60473.

Index of Peer Relationships (Hudson, 1982). This twenty-five-item self-report inventory, rated on a one-to-five continuum, measures the degree, severity, and magnitude of a client's problems in relationships with peers. It can be used as a global measure of peer relationship problems, or the practitioner can specify the peer reference group (i.e., work associates, friends). It is available from Richard D. Irwin, 181 Ridge Road, Homewood, IL 60473.

Maternal Characteristics Scale (Polansky, Gaudin, & Kilpatrick, 1992). This thirty-five-item observational rating scale consists of descriptive statements with which the caseworker assesses relatedness, impulse control, confidence, and verbal accessibility. Caseworkers respond to true or false (or mostly true/mostly false) questions. This scale is available from James M. Gaudin, PhD, University of Georgia, School of Social Work, Athens, GA 30602.

Michigan Screening Profile of Parenting (Paulson, Afifi, Chaleff, Thomason, & Liu, 1975). This thirty-item self-report inventory measures attitudes regarding child rearing and parental self-awareness and self-control. Clients respond to each item on a seven-point scale ranging from "strongly agree" to "strongly disagree." The profile is available from the Test Analysis and Development Corporation, 2400 Park Lake Drive, Boulder, CO 80301.

Nowicki-Strickland Locus of Control Scale (N-SLCS) (Nowicki & Strickland, 1973). This forty-item instrument is designed to assess a child's beliefs in chance or fate (external locus of control) or the influence of his or her own behavior (internal locus of control). It is targeted for children eleven to eighteen years of age and features items requiring a yes or no response. It is available from Dr. Stephen Nowicki, Jr., Department of Psychology, Emory University, Atlanta, GA 30322.

Problem-Oriented Screening Instrument for Teenagers (POSIT) (Rahdert, 1991). This 139-item self-report rating instrument assesses substance abuse problems, physical health status, mental health status, family relationships, peer relationships, educational status, vocational status, social skills, leisure and recreation, and aggressive behavior/delinquency. It is intended for use as a screening tool to identify problems in need of further assessment. It is available from the National Institute on Drug Abuse, 5600 Fishers Lane, Rockville, MD 20857.

Rosenberg Self-Esteem Scale (Rosenberg, 1979). This ten-item self-report inventory measures the self-esteem of high school students. Respondents rate each item on a four-point scale. This sacale is available from Morris Rosenberg, Department of Sociology, University of Maryland, College Park, MD 20742.

Self-Perception Profile for Children (Harter, 1982). This twenty-eight-item self-rating inventory assesses a child's perception of his or her cognitive, social, and physical competence. The scale is for use with children in the third through ninth grades. For each item, the child is asked first to identify which of two passages best describes him or her, and then rate whether the description is "sort of true" or "really true." This profile is available from Susan Harter, University of Denver, 2040 South York Street, Denver, CO 80208.

Family Level

The following assessment instruments focus on assessment at the familial level and address family functioning as well as marital relationships.

Attitude toward the Provision of Long-Term Care (Klein, 1992). This twenty-six-item self-report inventory, rated on a one-to-five continuum, measures attitudes toward the provision of informal long-term care for family members. It is available from Dr. Waldo Klein, School of Social Work, University of Connecticut, 1798 Asylum Avenue, West Hartford, CT 06117–2698.

Codependency Inventory (CODI) (Stonebrink, 1988). This twenty-nine-item instrument is designed to measure codependency in family and friends of substance abusers. Codependency is defined as enabling the abuser to continue to use chemicals and/or trying to control the abuser's use of alcohol and/or drugs. Items are responded to on a four-point continuum. This instrument is available from S. Stonebrink, School of Social Work, University of Hawaii, Honolulu, HI 96822.

Conflict Tactics Scale (Straus, 1979). This nineteen-item self-report inventory is widely used to assess conflict among family members. A parent or child responds on a six-point scale (from "never" to "more than 20 times") to indicate the number of times in the past year specific techniques were used during family conflict. This scale is available from Murray A. Strau, Director, Family Research Laboratory, University of New Hampshire, Durham, NH 03824-3586.

Dyadic Adjustment Scale (Spanier & Filsinger, 1983). This thirty-two-item self-report inventory, using three different types of rating responses, measures satisfaction in an intimate relationship. It is available as a chapter entitled "The Dyadic Adjustment Scale" in *Marriage and Family Assessment: A Source Book for Family Therapy*, edited by E. Filsinger (Beverly Hills: Sage).

Dyadic Parent–Child Interaction Coding System (Robinson & Eyberg, 1981). This observational procedure assesses the interaction of parents and young conduct-problem children. Parent and child are observed during 15-minute segments as they interact in three structured situations in a clinic playroom. It is available from Social and Behavior Science Documents, Select Press, PO Box 9838, San Raphael, CA 94912.

Family Adaptability and Cohesion Scale III (Olson, 1986). This forty-item self-report inventory assesses family cohesion, adaptability, and communication. Adults and children age twelve and older respond to each item on a five-point scale. The first half of the scale assesses how family members see their family (perceived), and the second half assesses how they would like it to be (ideal). This scale is available from Family Social Science, University of Minnesota, 297 McNeal Hall, St. Paul, MN 55108.

Family Assessment Form (McCroskey, Nishimoto, & Subramanian, 1991). This observational procedure includes five subscales with 102 items. The instrument assesses the family's physical, social, and economic environment; psychosocial history of caregivers; personal characteristics of caregivers; child-rearing skills; caregiver-to-child interactions; developmental status of children; and overall psychosocial functioning of the family from an ecological perspective. Family functioning is rated on a five-point Likert scale linked to child abuse and neglect. This instrument is available from the Children's Bureau of Los Angeles, 2824 Hyans Street, Los Angeles, CA 90026.

Index of Family Relations (Hudson, 1982). This twenty-five-item self-report inventory, rated on a one-to-five continuum, measures the extent, severity, or magnitude of problems that family members have in their relationships with one another. It is considered a global measure of family problems and is available from Richard D. Irwin, 181 Ridge Road, Homewood, IL 60473.

Index of Marital Satisfaction (Hudson, 1982). This twenty-five-item self-report inventory, using three different types of rating responses, measures the degree, severity, or magnitude of a problem one spouse or partner has in the marital relationship. It is available from Richard D. Irwin, 181 Ridge Road, Homewood, IL 60473.

Index of Spouse Abuse (Hudson & McIntosh, 1981). This thirty-item self-report scale, rated on a one-to-five continuum, measures the severity or magnitude of physical or nonphysical abuse inflicted on a woman by her spouse or partner. Clinical cutting scores are suggested for both physical or nonphysical abuse subscale scores. This index is available from Dr. Walter Hudson, University of Arizona, School of Social Work, Tempe, AZ 95287.

Inventory of Family Feelings (Lowman, 1980). This thirty-eight-item self-report inventory assesses the overall degree of attachment between each pair of family members. Family members with at least a sixth-grade education respond on a three-point scale to each item. This inventory is available from Joseph Lowman, Department of Psychology, CB# 3270 Davie Hall, University of North Carolina, Chapel Hill, NC 27511.

Marital Satisfaction Inventory (Snyder, 1983). This 280-item self-report inventory assesses individuals' attitudes and beliefs regarding eleven specific areas of marital relationship adjustment. It requires approximately 30 minutes for individual spouses to respond true or false on each item and includes subscales on dissatisfaction with children and conflict over child rearing. It is available from Western Psychological Services, 12031 Wilshire Boulevard, Los Angeles, CA 90025.

Parent–Adolescent Communications Inventory (Bienvenu, 1969). This forty-item self-report inventory assesses the patterns and characteristics of communication between parents and adolescents. Adolescents age thirteen and older respond to each item using a three-point scale. This inventory is available from Family Life Publications, Inc., Box 427, Saluda, NC 28773.

Parent–Child Behavioral Coding System (Forehand & McMahon, 1981). This observational procedure assesses patterns of parent–child interaction. An observer codes parent and child behaviors in a 10-minute structured exercise in a clinic and/or in a 40-minute unstructured home visit. This test is available as the publication *Helping the Noncompliant Child: A Clinician's Guide to Parental Training* (New York: Guilford Press, 1981).

Parent Locus of Control Scale (PLOC) (Campis, Lyman, & Prentice-Dunn, 1986). This forty-seven-item five-point scale is designed to measure parental locus of control relating to the parent's (internal) or child's (external) power in a given child-rearing situation. Items measure parental efficacy, parental responsibility, child's control of parents' life, parental belief in fate and chance, and parental control of child's behavior. This scale is available from Dr. Robert Lyman, Department of Psychology, University of Alabama, Box 870348, Tuscaloosa, AL 35487.

Parental Authority Questionnaire (PAQ) (Buri, 1991). This thirty-item instrument offers a five-point scale that is designed to measure parental authority and disciplinary practice. It is available from Dr. John R. Buri, Department of Psychology, University of St. Thomas, 2115 Summit Avenue, St. Paul, MN 55105.

Standardized Observation System 3 (Wahler, House, & Stambaugh, 1976). This observational procedure assesses interactions between a child and other members of a family. The observer codes the interactional sequence in a 1–hour unstructured home visit. This test is available from Austin Peay, University of Tennessee, Knoxville, TN 37996.

Environmental Level

The following assessment instruments focus on macrolevel analysis. Specifically, they are designed to assess factors critical to understanding the client's ecosystem.

Child Abuse Potential Survey (Milner, Gold, Ayoub, & Jacewitz, 1984). This 160-item self-report inventory, completed by a parent, is designed as a screening device to differentiate physical abusers from nonabusers. Factors measured include distress, rigidity, child with problems, problems from family and others, unhappiness, loneliness, and negative concepts of child and self. Respondents are asked to agree or disagree with each item. The inventory has a reliability level of grade three and includes a "lie scale" to identify individuals who tend to give socially desirable answers. It is available from Psytec, Inc., Box 564, DeKalb, IL 60115.

Child Well-Being Scales (Magura & Moses, 1986). These forty-three behavior-rating scales are a multidimensional measure of child maltreatment situations specifically designed for use as an outcome measure in child protective services programs rather than for individual case outcomes. Most of the scales focus on the actual or potential unmet needs of children. Current testing of the subscales indicates that three factors (household adequacy, ten scales; parental disposition, fourteen scales; and child performance, four scales) accounted for 43 percent variance and that the Child Well-Being Scale can discriminate between neglectful and nonneglectful families (Gaudin, Polansky, & Kilpatrick, 1992). Approximately 25 minutes are required for a service provider to complete the scales based on direct contact with the family, including in-home visits. Each dimension is rated on a three- or six-point continuum of adequacy/inadequacy. This instrument is available from the Publication Department, Child Welfare League of America, Suite 310, 440 First Street NW, Washington, DC 20001.

Childhood Level of Living Scale (Polansky, Chalmers, Buttenwieser, & Williams, 1981). This ninety-nine-item behavior-rating scale assesses neglect of children age seven and under. Nine subscales are general positive child care, state of repair of home, negligence, quality of household maintenance, quality of health care and grooming, encouragement of competence, inconsistency of discipline and coldness, encouragement of superego development, and material giving. Approximately 15 minutes are required for a service provider who knows the family well to answer all items yes or no. This scale is available from Norman A. Polansky, University of Georgia, School of Social Work, Athens, GA 30602.

Environmental Assessment Index (EAI) (Poresky, 1987). This forty-four-item instrument (or twenty-two-item short form) is designed to assess the educational/development quality of children's home environment. A home visitor scores each yes or no item based on either direct observation or information from the child's parent. This index is available as an article entitled "Environmental Assessment Index: Reliability, Stability and Validity of the Long and Short Forms," *Educational and Psychological Measurements, 47,* 969–975.

Family Inventory of Life Events and Changes (McCubbin & Patterson, 1983). This seventy-one-item self-report instrument records normative and nonnormative stressors a family unit may experience within a year. Adult family members (together or separately) respond yes or no to each item. Norms are provided for families at various stages in the family life cycle. This inventory is available from Family Social Science, 290 McNeal Hall, University of Minnesota, St. Paul, MN 55108.

Family Risk Scales (Magura, Moses, & Jones, 1987). These twenty-six behavior-rating scales are designed to identify a full range of situations predictive of near-term child placement so that preventive services can be offered and change can be monitored. The scales are similar in design, administration, and scoring to the Child Well-Being Scales. Dimensions are limited to the areas that are potentially malleable. This instrument is available from the Publication Department, Child Welfare League of America, Suite 310, 440 First Street NW, Washington, DC 20001–2085.

Home Observation for Measurement of the Environment Inventory (Caldwell & Bradley, 1978). This 100-item observation/interview procedure assesses the quality of stimulation of a child's early environment. There are two versions for children ages birth to three and one for three- to six-year-olds. Approximately one third of the items are answered through a parent interview; the remainder are based on observations of the child and the primary caretaker in the home. Approximately 1 hour is required to answer all of the questions yes or no. This inventory is available from Bettye M. Caldwell, Center for Child Development and Education, University of Arkansas at Little Rock, 33rd and University, Little Rock, AR 72204.

Inventory of Socially Supportive Behaviors (Barrera, Sandler, & Ramsay, 1981). This forty-item self-report inventory assesses the frequency with which individuals have received various forms of aid and assistance from the people around them. Respondents answer each item using a five-point scale (from "not at all" to "every day"). This inventory is available from Manuel Barrera, Jr., Department of Psychology, Arizona State University, Tempe, AZ 85287–1104.

Multiproblem Screening Inventory (MPSI) (Hudson, 1990). This 334-item self-report scale measures twenty-seven dimensions of family functioning. Subscales measure depression, self-esteem, partner problems, sexual discord, child problems, mother problems, personal stress, friend problems, neighbor problems, school problems, aggression, problems with work associates, family problems, suicide, nonphysical abuse, physical abuse, fearfulness, ideas of reference, phobias, guilt, work problems, confused thinking, disturbing thoughts, memory loss, alcohol abuse, and drug abuse. Questions are answered on a seven-point Likert scale (from "none of the time" to "all of the time"). The scale is easily computer scored to develop additional subscales and is available from WALMYR Publishing Co., PO Box 24779, Tempe, AZ 85285-4779.

Parenting Stress Index (Abidin, 1986). This 101-item self-report inventory assesses a mother's perception of stress associated with child and parent characteristics. An additional nineteen optional items assess life stress events. The index can be completed by mothers in approximately 20 to 30 minutes and is available from Pediatric Press, 2915 Idlewood Drive, Charlottesville, VA 22901.

Provision of Social Relations (PRS) (Turner, Frankel, & Levin, 1983). This fifteen-item instrument is designed to measure components of social support. The items are responded to on a five-point continuum. Social support consists of five components: attachment, social integration, reassurance of worth, reliable alliance, and guidance. This instrument is available, from the authors, as an article entitled "Social Support: Conceptualization, Measurement, and Implications for Mental Health," *Research in Community and Mental Health, 3*, 67–111.

Social Support Behaviors Scale (Vaux, Riedel, & Stewart, 1987). This forty-five-item self-report inventory measures five modes of support: emotional, socializing, practical assistance, financial assistance, and advice/guidance. Respondents record on a five-point scale (from "no one would do this" to "most family members/friends would certainly do this") the likelihood of family and friends helping in specific ways. This scale is available, from the authors, as an article entitled "Modes of Social Support: The Social Support Behaviors (SS-B) Scale," *American Journal of Community Psychology, 15,* 209–237.

CONCLUSION

There are a variety of assessment instruments available for assessing and treating a client's social functioning from an ecological perspective. The instruments presented in this chapter are a quantifiable means of assessment that can greatly improve the practitioner's effectiveness. The assessment instruments presented can be used for screening, treatment planning, monitoring, measuring client change, and evaluating outcome. These instruments are inexpensive, involve little time to administer, and are generally easy to score and interpret. They are tools that will greatly improve the assessment and treatment process and ultimately improve the lives of clients.

REFERENCES

Abidin, R. R. (1986). *Parenting Stress Index manual.* Charlottesville, VA: Pediatric Psychology Press.

Achenbach, T. M., & Edelbrock, C. S. (1979). The Child Behavior Profile: II. Boys aged 12–16 and girls aged 6–11 and 12–16. *Journal of Consulting and Clinical Psychology, 47,* 223–233.

Alpern, G. D., Boll, T. J., & Shearer, M. W. (1980). *The Developmental Profile II manual.* Aspen, CO: Psychological Development.

Barrera, M., Jr., Sandler, I. N., & Ramsay, T. B. (1981). Preliminary development of a scale of social support: Studies on college students. *American Journal of Community Psychology, 9,* 435–447.

Bavolek, S. J. (1984). *Handbook for the Adult–Adolescent Parenting Inventory.* Schaumberg, IL: Family Development Associates.

Beck, A. T. (1967). *Depression: Clinical, experimental and theoretical aspects.* New York: Harper & Row.

Bienvenu, M. J. (1969). Measurement of parent–adolescent communication. *Family Coordinator, 19,* 117–121.

Birleson, P. (1981). The validity of depression disorders in childhood and the development of a self-rating scale: A research report. *Journal of Child Psychology and Psychiatry, 22,* 73–88.

Buri, J. R. (1991). Parental Authority Questionnaire. *Journal of Personality and Social Assessment, 57*, 110–119.

Caldwell, B. M., & Bradley, R. H. (1978). *Home observation for measurement of the environment*. Little Rock: University of Arkansas.

Campis, L. K., Lyman, R. D., & Prentice-Dunn, S. (1986). The Parental Locus of Control Scale: Development and validation. *Journal of Clinical Child Psychiatry, 15*, 260–267.

Forehand, R. L., & McMahon, R. J. (1981). *Helping the noncompliant child: A clinician's guide to parent training*. New York: Guilford Press.

Gaudin, J. M., Polansky, N. A., & Kilpatrick, A. C. (1992). The Child Well-Being Scales: A field trial. *Child Welfare, 71*(4), 319–328.

Harter, S. (1982). The Perceived Competence Scale for Children. *Child Development, 53*, 87–97.

Honig, A. S., Caldwell, B. M., & Tannenbaum, J. A. (1973). Maternal behavior in verbal report and in laboratory observation: A methodological study. *Child Psychiatry and Human Development, 3*, 216–230.

Hudson, W. W. (1982). *The clinical measurement package: A field manual*. Chicago: Dorsey Press.

_____. (1990). *The Multiproblem Screening Inventory*. Tempe, AZ: WALMYR.

Hudson, W. W., & McIntosh, S. R. (1981). The assessment of spouse abuse: Two quantifiable dimensions. *Journal of Marriage and the Family, 43*, 873–888.

Humphreys, L. L. (1982). Children's and teacher's perspectives on children's self-control: The development of two rating scales. *Journal of Consulting and Clinical Psychology, 50*, 624–633.

Humphreys, L. L., & Ciminero, A. R. (1979). Parent report measures of child behavior: A review. *Journal of Clinical Child Psychology, 8*, 56–63.

Klein, W. C. (1992). Measuring caregiver attitude toward the provision of long-term care. *Journal of Social Service Research, 16*, 147–162.

Kovacs, M. (1981). Rating scales to assess depression in school-aged children. *Acta Paedopsychiatrica, 46*, 305–315.

Kurdek, L. A., & Berg, B. (1987). Children's Beliefs about Parental Divorce Scale: Psychometric characteristics and concurrent validity. *Journal of Consulting and Clinical Psychology, 55*, 712–718.

Lowman, J. (1980). Measurement of family affective structure. *Journal of Personality Assessment, 44*, 130–141.

Magura, A., Moses, B. S., & Jones, M. A. (1987). *Assessing risk and measuring change in families: The Family Risk Scales*. Washington, DC: Child Welfare League of America.

Magura, A., & Moses, B. S. (1986). *Outcome measures for child welfare services: Theory and applications.* Washington, DC: Child Welfare League of America.

Mayer, J., & Filstead, W. J. (1979). The Adolescent Alcohol Involvement Scale: An instrument for measuring adolescents' use and misuse of alcohol. *Journal of Studies in Alcohol, 40,* 291–300.

McCroskey, J., Nishimoto, R., & Subramanian, K. (1991). Assessment in family support programs: Initial reliability and validity testing of the Family Assessment Form. *Child Welfare, 70*(1), 19–33.

McCubbin, H. I., & Patterson, J. M. (1983). Stress: The Family Inventory of Life Events and Changes. In E. E. Filsinger (Ed.), *Marriage and family assessment: A sourcebook for family therapy* (pp. 275–297). Beverly Hills, CA: Sage.

Milner, J. S., Gold, R. G., Ayoub, C., & Jacewitz, M. M. (1984). Predictive validity of the Child Abuse Potential Inventory. *Journal of Consulting and Clinical Psychology, 52,* 879–884.

Nowicki, S., & Strickland, B. R. (1973). A locus of control scale for children. *Journal of Consulting and Clinical Psychology, 40,* 148–154.

Olson, D. H. (1986). Circumplex Model Seven: Validation studies and FACES III. *Family Process, 25,* 337–351.

Paulson, M., Afifi, A. A., Chaleff, A., Thomason, M. L., & Liu, V. Y. (1975). An MMPI scale for identifying "at risk" abusive parents. *Journal of Clinical Child Psychology, 4,* 22–24.

Polansky, N. A., Chalmers, M. A., Buttenwieser, E., & Williams, D. P. (1981). *Damaged parents: An anatomy of child neglect.* Chicago: University of Chicago Press.

Polansky, N. A., Gaudin, J. M., & Kilpatrick, A. C. (1992). The Maternal Characteristics Scale: A cross validation. *Child Welfare, 71*(3), 271–280.

Poresky, R. H. (1987). Environmental Assessment Index: Reliability, stability and validity of the long and short forms. *Educational and Psychological Measurements, 47,* 969–975.

Quay, H. C. (1977). Measuring dimensions of deviant behavior: The Behavior Problem Checklist. *Journal of Abnormal Child Psychology, 5,* 277–287.

Rahdert, E. R. (Ed.). (1991). *The adolescent assessment/referral system manual.* Washington, DC: United States Department of Health and Human Services.

Robinson, E. A., & Eyberg, S. M. (1981). The dyadic parent–child interaction coding system: Standardization and validation. *Journal of Counseling and Clinical Psychology, 49,* 245–250.

Rosenberg, M. (1979). *Conceiving the self.* New York: Basic Books.

Snyder, D. K. (1983). Clinical and research applications of the Marital Satisfaction Inventory. In E. E. Filsinger (Ed.), *Marriage and family assessment: A sourcebook for family therapy* (pp. 169–198). Beverly Hills, CA: Sage.

Spanier, G. B., & Filsinger, E. E. (1983). The Dyadic Adjustment Scale. In E. E. Filsinger (Ed.), *Marriage and family assessment: A sourcebook for family therapy* (pp. 155–168). Beverly Hills, CA: Sage.

Stonebrink, S. (1988). *A measure of co-dependency and the impact of socio-cultural characteristics.* Unpublished master's thesis, University of Hawaii School of Social Work.

Straus, M. A. (1979). Measuring intrafamily conflict and violence: The Conflict Tactics (CT) Scales. *Journal of Marriage and the Family, 41,* 75–88.

Turner, R. J., Frankel, B. G., & Levin, D. M. (1983). Social support: Conceptualization, measurement, and implications for mental health. *Research in Community Mental Health, 3,* 67–111.

Vaux, A., Riedel, S., & Stewart, D. (1987). Modes of social support: The Social Support Behaviors (SS-B) Scale. *American Journal of Community Psychology, 15,* 209–237.

Wahler, R. G., House, A. E., & Stambaugh, E. E. (1976). *Ecological assessment of child problem behavior.* New York: Pergamon Press.

Wodarski, J. S. (1981). *The role of research in clinical practice: A practical approach for the human services.* Baltimore, MD: University Park Press.

Zatz, S., & Chassing, L. (1983). Cognitions of test-anxious children. *Journal of Consulting and Clinical Psychology, 51,* 526–534.

Chapter 9

Ecological Assessment and Intervention

Kurt Lewin (1951) concluded that there is nothing so practical as theory to guide one's view of the social world. Keeping Lewin's maxim in mind, practitioners can use ecological theory as a useful perspective to assess problems of clients and treat these problems in a holistic fashion.

The link between ecology and problematic social functioning has been documented in relationships between differences in social organization of communities and suicide rates, between social class and psychiatric hospitalization, and between the spatial pattern of a community and the probability of certain kinds of mental illness (Nathan & Harris, 1975). Szasz (1961) points out that problems in client functioning (e.g., those who are emotionally troubled) arise not when persons commit certain acts but when the act becomes known to some other person, who then defines or labels the act as disturbed. Newbrough (1971) argues that this labeling occurs with clear reference to the ecological context.

As noted in earlier chapters, the connection between ecosystems and persons who are emotionally troubled can be conceptualized within a main-effects framework (bad environments cause emotional disturbance) or within a transactional framework (the interaction of bad environment and personal characteristics helps create emotional disturbance; Sameroff, 1975). The adoption of a transactional framework advances the practitioner's understanding of the relationship between the ecosystem and social functioning. Samer-off concludes that the underlying assumption of the transactional model is that the contact between organism and environment is a transaction in which each is altered by the other. Sameroff provides an excellent example:

The mother who comes to label her infant as "difficult" may come to treat the child as difficult irrespective of his or her actual behavior. (T)he child . . . will come to accept difficulty as one of the central elements in his or her self-image, thereby indeed becoming the "difficult" child for all time. (p. 100)

The process of transaction has been useful for providing insight into the relationship between child abuse and emotionally troubled children and even into the development of schizophrenia. Sameroff and Chandler (1975) found, in a review of the literature on child abuse, that attempts to isolate linear cause-effect relationships between abuse and emotionally troubled children have been largely futile. They point out that although abused children have been presumed to be passive recipients of negative environmental influences, these children in some situations have been shown to exhibit a variety of negative behaviors that influence the process of abuse. Thus, they see the potential for understanding child abuse in terms of a mutual influence in which the parent and child are partners.

Sameroff and Zax (1978), in a longitudinal study of schizo-phrenic women and their children, found evidence of the transac-tional process. They found no evidence that schizophrenia had been transmitted linearly during the first $2\frac{1}{2}$ years of the child's life. This led them to conclude that the intellectual incompetence of the young infant makes it highly unlikely that he or she can learn the schizophrenic facts of life. As the child grows in cognitive and linguistic skill, he or she becomes increasingly competent at iden-tifying and adapting to the craziness in his or her social environ-ment. Gradually the child learns to make increasingly significant contributions to the schizophrenic transactions with the mother, and evidence of problematic behavior in the child begins to mani-fest itself across larger numbers of ecological contexts. The child judged to be the most troubled is the one who unfortunately arouses disturbed reactions in those around him or her in more than one ecological setting (Hobbs, 1966).

The ecological perspective requires a shift in theory by those who come out of a traditional social work perspective. The shift is away from individual pathology and toward an understanding of a unit defined as individual-in-the-ecology. The practitioner may view problems in social functioning as learned patterns that may be understandable responses to a maladaptive social system. The practitioner who uses the ecological perspective in practice should be concerned with traditional labels that define the client as emotionally disturbed. A more accurate label would be the "disturbing client," one that better communicates the transactional nature of the reciprocity between client and ecology (Hobbs, 1980).

AN ECOLOGICAL STRATEGY OF ASSESSMENT AND INTERVENTION

An important prerequisite for social intervention is an ecological assessment of the client's presenting problem(s). Ecological assessment includes two major issues:

1. Identifying sources of discord in the client's ecosystem as well as sources of strengths that can be used to improve the goodness-of-fit between the client and important people in the client's life

2. Specifying what services and other social treatment are required to enable the client to make progress toward the achievement of treatment goals (Hobbs, 1980).

Traditional models of social work assessment and intervention, when compared to the ecological approach, are far more narrow and view the individual client as the primary focus of the assessment and treatment process (Germain, 1973). The intervention model presented in Chapter 1 is reiterated in this section. This chapter provides a brief discussion of each of the steps of the assessment and intervention process. As noted in Chapter 1, the treatment model that follows can be referred to as an ecosystem-oriented assessment-intervention approach, adapted from the field of community psychology (Plas, 1981).

The ecosystem-oriented assessment-intervention approach involves seven stages and can be used in a variety of practice settings. The model does not deviate a great deal from traditional approaches to assessment and intervention in terms of data gathering, but rather in the way that the practitioner conceptualizes and organizes the assessment and intervention process. The seven stages are as follows:

1. Entering the system
2. Mapping the ecology
3. Assessing the ecology
4. Creating the vision of change
5. Coordinating and communicating
6. Reassessing
7. Evaluating.

Entering the System

Once the decision has been made to offer services to a client, the first step the practitioner takes is to enter the ecosystem of the client. This process involves two major steps: (1) assessment of the relationships in the client's life and (2) identification of a point of entry into the client's world. Assessing the relationships of the client involves focusing on the subsystems that shape the client's world; these include the family, the school, and the community. The practitioner gathers critical input from these subsystems that will guide the intervention process. The next step for the practitioner is to find a point of entry into the client's world. This can be accomplished through an interview involving the client and his or her family. If the client is a child, the interview might be accomplished through attending an already-scheduled meeting between parent and teacher. Through assessing the various subsystems in the client's world, the practitioner is able to identify sources of discord in the client's ecosystem, as well as strengths.

Mapping the Ecology

After the practitioner enters the client's world, the next step involves the process of mapping the ecology. Systems analysis is a critical strategy during this stage. The practitioner analyzes various subsystems of the client's world to identify the people and events pertinent to the presenting problem(s) of the client.

Important subsystems related to the client can be classified in two broad categories: people and events. Events of importance include those considered to be typical occasions within the client's world that support either positive or negative behaviors and feelings. These events are identified through interaction and discussion with representatives of the various subsystems in the client's ecosystem. For example, the husband of the client may state during an interview, "Whenever she is around the children, she acts as if I don't exist" or "When we are away from the children, our relationship seems to be fuller." These statements provide insight into the subsystem of the mother and children within the larger family systems. The comment suggests that the interaction between the husband and wife changes when the children are present. This kind of information is critical to the assessment process.

Identification of people and events can be accomplished through a number of approaches, including structured interviews with the client and significant persons in the client's life. A number of empirically based assessment instruments are available that can provide information relevant to the client's presenting problem(s). Examples of these instruments are reviewed in Chapter 8. Hudson (1982), in particular, has created a number of scales that can be used to assess relationships in family systems; these instruments are the Index of Family Relations, Child's Attitude toward Mother, Child's Attitude toward Father, and Parental Attitude Scale. Conducting a Social Support Network can be a useful tool for mapping the client's ecosystem (Plas, 1981). Family sculpturing can also be a useful tool for mapping family problems (Hartman, 1976).

Assessing the Ecology

Once the ecology has been mapped, the data gathered must be interpreted. At this point, the practitioner is searching for the primary problems and the major areas of strength in the client's ecosystem. An important component of this stage is to describe relationships and recurring themes in the client's ecosystem.

Relationships between influential events and influential persons present at those events need to be assessed, and recurring themes need to be recorded. For example, is the same person, or group of persons, always present at those events that are deemed critical? Which events are viewed as influential by more than one or two significant persons in the client's ecosystem? These kinds of data allow the practitioner to assign weights to those relationships that appear to be important. Those events and persons mentioned most often are considered to have the greatest influence with respect to maintaining the ecosystem of the client as well as the possibilities for changing it.

The process is designed to elicit data concerning those people and situations that support useful behaviors and those that support negative actions and feelings. Once the strengths, weaknesses, and critical relationships have been identified, the practitioner can present this information to the client and significant persons in the client's ecosystem. The most central stage of the social treatment process is next.

Creating the Vision of Change

At this point in the process, the benefits of assessing and mapping the ecology begin to be realized. This phase of the intervention process includes all of those significant individuals in the client's ecosystem that can influence change. Through this contact, the practitioner stresses the areas that need to be changed to enhance the client's social functioning.

When focusing on the changes needed, the practitioner must consider the total ecosystem of the client and build on the strengths present in this ecology. The practitioner should be sensitive to all possibilities of change. When significant persons (and, in particular, the client) have agreed to the intervention plan, the next stage is to implement it.

Coordinating and Communicating

An important activity of the practitioner during the intervention process is to coordinate and communicate with those in the client's ecosystem. For the most part, much of the change effort is the responsibility of the significant persons in the client's ecosystem. Simply put, the practitioner offers support and facilitates the continuing change efforts through such behaviors as home visits, telephone calls, and other support efforts. Given that the client's ecosystem is dynamic, the practitioner must be open to the possibility that the intervention efforts may have to be modified and changed. This is the focus of the next stage.

Reassessing

Based on the agreed-on change by the client and the significant persons in the client's ecosystem, the practitioner must be open to the need to remap the client's ecosystem and work through subsequent stages of the intervention process. Exploration of this possibility is accomplished through the traditional assessment method of interviewing the client and others in the client's ecosystem and by using those technologies discussed in Chapter 8. If the intervention efforts are assessed to be successful, the practitioner can move toward the termination process with the client and other significant persons in the client's ecosystem.

Evaluating

Whereas the reassessment phase is concerned with outcomes, this final stage of intervention is concerned with the total evaluation of the entire treatment process. The practitioner can gather information through informal meetings with the client and others relevant to the treatment process, or this evaluation can be done through a structured questionnaire and other research technologies. The total evaluation of the treatment process is important because it helps the practitioner improve the ecosystem-oriented assessment-intervention treatment approach.

A CASE EXAMPLE

Gary, a two-year-old boy, was underdeveloped both physically and intellectually. The child's vocabulary consisted of approximately three words, and he was not able to walk more than two steps without assistance. The child was diagnosed as having fetal alcohol syndrome. The symptoms included syndactyly (fusion of the fingers) of the middle and ring fingers bilaterally, and other evidence of fetal alcohol syndrome was also present. Gary's parents were both alcoholics and unemployed when Gary was placed in foster care. The family was not receiving any kind of public assistance.

The worker assigned to Gary's case had his first opportunity to enter the ecosystem of Gary during a 2–hour home visit with his parents while a number of relatives were also present. The worker observed the interaction patterns between Gary and the family.

During the home visit, the worker began the stage of mapping the ecology of Gary's family system. The worker concluded that Gary's parents did not interact with him in a typical fashion. The mother, in particular, held the child for no more than 2 minutes during the home visit, and the father did not interact with the child at all. When the child was not playing on the floor, he was passed from one relative to the next. The mother commented several times during the home visit about how curious Gary had always been about things in his environment and how active the child was. These comments were totally out of touch with the child's physical and intellectual behavior.

One week after the visit, the worker did an extensive interview with each of the parents and one of the relatives present at the home visit a week earlier. Gathering this information helped the caseworker assess the ecological system of the child and the intervention needed to help Gary return to his biological family. Through the interview, the worker learned that both parents continued to abuse alcohol; this was confirmed by Gary's parents and the relative interviewed. It was also learned that Gary's father was working part time and had not reported this income to Family Services. The worker viewed the fact that Gary's father was working as a strength even though the income earned was not reported.

The next step, creating the vision of change, involved a number of services and persons in Gary's ecosystem. The worker had to coordinate each of these services to ensure that the change effort was being followed through. It was decided that Gary should continue in foster care for two more months before his case review. During this time, Gary would go into a special treatment program aimed at increasing Gary's motor and intellectual development. Since the child was underweight and in the lower fifth percentile in height, regular visits to a medical doctor were prescribed. The worker also instructed the foster parents to provide a stimulating environment for the child.

Gary's parents agreed to attend counseling for treatment of their alcohol problem. They also agreed to participate in parenting classes and were linked with other social services in the community. The worker closely monitored the parent's activities to ensure that they followed through on the agreed plan. An effort was made to help Gary's father find a full-time job. The coordinating-communicating stage was accomplished through telephone calls and home visits. The parents also agreed that when Gary visited each week for 2 hours, they would not have relatives present. This strategy was used to help the worker assess how the parents alone interacted with Gary.

After 2 months, the reassessment stage began. Gary's motor and intellectual development had improved through the efforts of the specialized treatment program and those of the foster parents. Gary was now able to walk alone and had a significant increase in his vocabulary. Gary's mother had followed through on her counseling for alcoholism; however, his father had missed a number of sessions. Gary's parents had also attended parenting classes on a regular basis. Gary's father found full-time employment. Since the income earned by Gary's father was extremely low, the family was eligible for a number of social services, including low-rent housing. During Gary's weekly 2–hour home visits, only Gary's parents were present, and the worker observed much improvement. Adequate housing was obtained by the family, and the family began receiving important social services.

It was the opinion of the alcohol counselor that Gary's mother was making great progress; however, she was not deemed ready for Gary to return home. There was also some concern about Gary's father's not attending counseling on a regular basis. The professionals working with Gary, including the medical doctor, felt that

Gary should continue to receive specialized treatment to improve his physical and emotional development. Thus it was decided that Gary should continue in foster care for two additional months. Gary's parents agreed to this plan. They would continue counseling, home visits would occur on a weekly basis for 2 hours, and Gary would continue receiving the necessary treatment. The final evaluation step was not implemented because intervention efforts were still in process (Pardeck, 1988).

CONCLUSION

The ecological perspective defines human problems as the outcomes of transaction between environments and people. Conceptualizing human problems in this fashion helps draw attention to the traditional concerns of social work practice, which go back to Mary Richmond, who realized that a disjunction between the person and the environment could exert a negative impact on people physically, emotionally, and socially. Germain (1979) points out that this focus is the distinguishing and unifying characteristic of social work practice.

Even though the ecological perspective helps practitioners conceptualize the traditional concerns of social work practice, Conte and Halpin (1983) have noted that it still has a number of inherent problems. It has not provided a clear set of procedures for (1) assessment, (2) intervention techniques, or (3) strategies and rationales for their use.

Others have pointed out that when the practitioner intervenes in the ecosystem of the client, the rippling and reverberating effects of intervention are not always clear in terms of outcome. Unintended and negative consequences are a common result of planned systematic change efforts. A classic example of this is the deinstitutionalization of mental hospital patients, which has resulted in the dumping of severely handicapped and incompetent people into hostile communities and in revolving-door types of treatment experiences for such people (Scull, 1977).

Another limitation of an ecological approach to treatment is that it encourages practitioners to see problems in such a broad-based fashion that they feel they must be experts not only in psychotherapy but also in family therapy, community practice, and so forth.

In a certain sense, the practitioner attempts to think and plan in such a comprehensive fashion that practice effectiveness can be jeopardized (Brawley, 1978).

Even though the foregoing arguments have merit and clearly need to be considered, an ecological approach to practice has much to offer social workers now (Hartman, 1970). In particular, it enables practitioners to gain a larger perspective and a dynamic understanding of people and their social, cultural, and physical milieu. We understand more clearly, for example, how dysfunctional behavior of a child can help maintain the pathological balance of a family system. Other factors, including social class, ethnicity, economic factors, and social institutional organizations (such as school and family) have a powerful affect on the lives of clients and their families. Such a perspective avoids blaming the victim and locates the assessment and treatment of the problem in the client's ecosystem (Siporin, 1980).

The ecosystem-oriented assessment-intervention approach borrowed from the field of community psychology obviously does not solve all the problems of the ecological perspective, as pointed out by Conte and Halpin (1983) and others. However, it does offer clearly defined stages around which the practitioner can organize assessment and intervention. It also emphasizes the importance of ongoing assessment procedures, ranging from the traditional interviewing approach to the newer clinical indexes being developed for practice. Most important, the model stresses the need to conceptualize and organize the assessment and intervention process at each stage of treatment from an ecological perspective. This may be the model's most redeeming quality.

REFERENCES

Brawley, E. A. (1978). Maximizing the potential of the social work team. *Journal of Sociology and Social Welfare, 5,* 731–743.

Conte, J., & Halpin, T. (1983). New services for families. In A. Rosenblatt & D. Waldfogel (Eds.), *Handbook of clinical social work* (pp. 20–25). San Francisco: Jossey-Bass.

Germain, C. (1973). An ecological perspective in casework. *Social Casework, 54,* 323–330.

———. (1979). *Social work practice: People and environments.* New York: Columbia University Press.

Hartman, A. (1976). *Finding families: An ecological approach to family assessment in adoption.* Beverly Hills, CA: Sage.

———. (1970). To think about the unthinkable. *Social Casework, 50,* 467–474.

Hobbs, N. (1966). Helping disturbed children: Psychological and ecological strategies. *American Psychologist, 21,* 1105–1115.

———. (1980). An ecologically oriented, service-based system for the classification of handicapped children. In S. Salzinger, J. Antrobus, & J. Glick (Eds.), *The ecosystem of the "sick" child: Implications for classification and intervention for disturbed and mentally retarded children* (pp. 28–42). New York: Academic Press.

Hudson, W. (1982). *The clinical measurement package: A field manual.* Homewood, IL: The Dorsey Press.

Lewin, K. (1951). *Field theory in social science.* New York: Harper & Brothers.

Nathan, P., & Harris, S. (1975). *Psychopathology and society.* New York: McGraw-Hill.

Newbrough, J. R. (1971). Behavioral perspectives on psychosocial classification. *American Journal of Orthopsychiatry, 42,* 843–845.

Pardeck, J. T. (1988). Social treatment through an ecological approach. *Clinical Social Work Journal, 16,* 92–104.

Plas, J. (1981). The psychologist in the school community: A liaison role. *School Psychology Review, 10,* 72–81.

Sameroff, A. (1975). Transactional models in early social relations. *Human Development, 18,* 65–79.

Sameroff, A., & Chandler, M. (1975). Reproductive risk and the continuum of caretaking causality. In D. Horowitz, E. M. Hetherington, S. Scarr-Slapstek, & G. M. Siegel (Eds.), *Review of child development research* (Vol. 20, pp. 201–212). Chicago, IL: University of Chicago Press.

Sameroff, A., & Zax, A. (1978). A search of schizophrenia: Young offspring of schizophrenic women. In L. Wynne (Ed.), *The nature of schizophrenic women* (pp. 430–441). New York: Wiley.

Scull, A. T. (1977). *Decarceration.* Englewood Cliffs, NJ: Prentice-Hall.

Siporin, M. (1980). Ecological systems theory in social work. *Journal of Sociology and Social Welfare, 7,* 507–532.

Szasz, T. (1961). *The myth of mental illness.* New York: Harper & Row.

Chapter 10

The Americans with Disabilities Act and Advocacy

On July 26, 1990, President Bush signed the Americans with Disabilities Act (ADA) into law. This legislation is referred to as the "emancipation proclamation for people with disabilities" because of its great importance for disabled members of American society. As the new law is implemented and enforced, it will have significant implications for all citizens. For local governments, changes are required in countless ordinances, building codes, and policies. For private industry, new provisions must be implemented in the workplace. These include hiring procedures, job restructuring, work schedules, training materials and equipment, and other factors affecting workers with disabilities. In essence, the ADA extends the same protections for people with disabilities to those found for other minorities under the Civil Rights Act of 1964.

PHILOSOPHIES DEFINING DISABILITIES

Before reviewing the reasons for the Americans with Disabilities Act and its key provisions, one must understand that social policies with respect to people with disabilities are the result of historical processes. These historical processes have been guided by three general philosophies: utilitarianism, humanitarianism, and human rights. These philosophies developed during different historical eras and reflect the thinking of each time period. All three philosophies have had significant influence on social policy affecting people with disabilities (Pardeck & Chung, 1992).

Utilitarianism

The major theme of utilitarianism is that usefulness determines the value of a person or thing to society (Sussman, 1965). Obviously, the utility of a person or thing is unique to each given society; however, the core criterion for usefulness has always been the greatest good or happiness for the greatest number of people in a given society. Usefulness had a much different meaning among primitive societies versus modern societies. In primitive societies, the person with a disability was often seen as a burden to the social group because he or she could not contribute to the welfare of the group. During times of severe hardship, persons with disabilities were simply abandoned or killed. Even though the expression of the utilitarian philosophy among many primitive societies would be considered barbaric and cruel by most modern-day societies, it was regarded by those primitive societies as a necessity for survival (Pardeck & Chung, 1992).

Primitive societies had a narrow view of the world. They viewed disability as the work of evil spirits and specifically as an expression of the disfavor of the gods. The person with disabilities was often seen as a hazard to primitive societies and thus sacrificed to appease the gods (Brothwell & Sandison, 1967; Galdston, 1963). These beliefs about people with disabilities persisted into the Middle Ages (Newman, 1987).

The development of Christianity brought about possibilities for improved treatment of the disabled; however, in practice little changed. Even into the Middle Ages, disabilities continued to be viewed as a consequence of original sin and a sign of God's disfavor. People were seen in terms of good and evil; persons with disabilities were largely viewed as evil (Newman, 1987). Yet even within the primitive world, there was ambiguity of regard for persons with disabilities, particularly for malformed infants, who were preserved and worshipped as awe-inspiring objects (Fiedler, 1978). Such ambiguities are seen as the origins of present-day conflictual attitudes toward disabilities, which all too frequently result in policies of segregation, isolation, and discrimination (Pardeck & Chung, 1992).

Humanitarianism

During the Renaissance, the Church established a more enlightened view of human life: that all life was sacred. However, the principal focus of early Christianity on a future heavenly life, distinct from a present earthly one, did not lead to significant changes in the treatment of people with disabilities. Nascent forces, however, emerged during the Renaissance and evolved into the philosophy of humanitarianism. The humanitarian philosophy attached central importance to the well-being of all people: Each person has worth and is not subordinated to political and biological theories. Given this enlightened view, new thought emerged in all fields, particularly the arts, politics, literature, architecture, and sciences. The core principles of humanistic philosophy emerged from these sources (Pardeck & Chung, 1992).

Unfortunately, during the Renaissance, most persons with disabilities did not survive to adulthood. Furthermore, the societies of the Western world had neither the infrastructure nor the capabilities and resources to cope with the overwhelming numbers of persons with disabilities. These conditions would not change until the late nineteenth century. Gradually the growth of wealth in the Western world led to advanced knowledge and technology, and these advances softened the harsh view of utilitarian philosophy. Out of these conditions emerged the humanitarian movement (Pardeck & Chung, 1992).

Along with the humanitarian treatment of people with disabilities in the nineteenth century, a competing theme, Social Darwinism, also emerged. Social Darwinism created attitudes of indifference toward people with disabilities. The disabled were simply viewed as unfit, and thus not caring for people with disabilities was justified under the tenets of this philosophy. The principal beliefs of eugenicists evolved from Social Darwinism. For persons with disabilities, the eugenicists advocated euthanasia, prohibition of marriage, segregation, and sterilization (Pardeck & Chung, 1992).

   Legislation toward these goals began in 1897, and by the 1930s, twenty-eight states had created sterilization laws (Burgdorf & Burgdorf, 1977). Laws banning persons with disabilities from appearing in public were also common in the early 1900s (Ianacone, 1977). For example, in 1900 the city of Chicago had an ordinance called "The Ugly Law," which prevented persons with disabilities from appearing on the streets. In 1919, a Wisconsin school board expelled a cerebral palsy student, even though the student was keeping up with his studies, because the students and school personnel found the student repulsive (Pardeck & Chung, 1992).

   Many of the punitive laws concerning the disabled were challenged as being unconstitutional. One notable case, *Buck v. Bell,* reached the Supreme Court in 1927. The Supreme Court found *Buck v. Bell* constitutional, thus making it legal to sterilize the mentally disabled. However, *Buck v. Bell* was one of many cases ultimately challenged within the legal system (Hull, 1977).

   Into the twentieth century, the emphasis on caring for people with disabilities was largely viewed as a problem relegated to private humanitarian groups. Their focus was largely on the creation of institutions to care for the impaired. Such institutional treatment posed numerous problems, including the negative psychological and social problems resulting from institutionalized care for people with disabilities. It became apparent that the power and resources of government must be involved to correct the limited efforts by private humanitarian groups and, in particular, the negative effects of Social Darwinism (Pardeck & Chung, 1992).

Human Rights Philosophy

   The philosophy of human rights is reflected through law, specifically in the United States Constitution, the Bill of Rights, and the Fifth and Fourteenth Amendments of the Constitution, which guarantee rights, equal protection, and due process. The human rights perspective does have elements of the humanitarian philosophy, with its emphasis on the intrinsic value of the individual. What separates the humanitarian philosophy from the human rights perspective, however, is that the intrinsic worth of the individual is protected by law (Pardeck & Chung, 1992).

Human rights for people with disabilities were influenced by the allied civil and minority rights movements. As in the minority rights struggle, the focus was largely on the right to a public education. Public education for children with disabilities was limited, and most were excluded from the mainstream education environment. The challenge to this exclusion began with the 1954 *Brown v. The Board of Education* case on behalf of African American children. The decision, handed down in 1954, was grounded in the Fourteenth Amendment, which guarantees everyone equal protection under the law. Under this law, what is done for some people must be done for all persons on equal terms unless there is a compelling reason for differential treatment. Thus the rationale for equal educational opportunity was established by the *Brown v. The Board of Education* ruling. Furthermore, states cannot set up separate systems and procedures for dealing with the disabled that differ from those for the able (Newman, 1987). In essence, the result has been that the disabled child has a right to the same education received by the able child (Pardeck & Chung, 1992).

Legal efforts in earlier years helped establish the present-day movement toward the deinstitutionalization and integration of people with disabilities in the larger society. These earlier legal efforts influenced three major federal laws in the 1970s: the Education for All Handicapped Children Act (P.L. 94-142, 1975); Title V (Section 504), Rehabilitation Amendments of 1973 (P.L. 93–112); and the Developmentally Disabled Assistance and Bill of Rights Act (P.L. 94-103, 1975). All three laws are grounded in the human rights philosophy and essentially afforded these statutory safeguards: (1) accessibility to programs and facilities supported by or operated by the federal government, (2) protection against discrimination in federally assisted programs, and (3) the right to a free and appropriate education (Pardeck & Chung, 1992).

SPECIFICS OF THE AMERICANS WITH DISABILITIES ACT

The ADA is grounded in the human rights philosophy. It is based on the position that people with disabilities have not received the same treatment as others and that it is the responsibility of the state to affirm or reaffirm those rights through judicial and legislative actions. The humanitarian philosophy also comes through in the

ADA because people with disabilities are viewed as having intrinsic worth and dignity. The utilitarian view also has limited influence on the ADA; for example, employers must make reasonable accommodations to assist people with disabilities in the workplace. However, employers can argue that an accommodation is unreasonable because of excessive costs. In other words, the cost for accommodating the person with a disability cannot necessarily outweigh the benefits. The utilitarian perspective always stresses the practicality and cost effectiveness of programs (Pardeck & Chung, 1992).

Findings Supporting Need for the ADA

The ADA (P.L. Law 101–336, 1990) was signed into law based on the following findings:

1. There are forty-three million Americans who have one or more physical or mental disabilities.

2. Historically, society has tended to isolate and segregate the disabled.

3. Discrimination in the areas of employment, housing, public accommodations, transportation, and education has been an incredible deterrent in the implementation of the rights of the disabled.

4. Discrimination on the basis of disability frequently has had no legal recourse.

5. Individuals with disabilities are intentionally excluded by architectural, transportation, or communication barriers and practices that result in lesser opportunities.

6. People with disabilities as a group occupy inferior status and are disadvantaged socially, vocationally, economically, and educationally.

7. Individuals with disabilities are a distinct and insular minority who have been faced with restrictions and limitations and subjected to unequal treatment.

8. The nation's proper goals should be to assure equality of opportunity, full participation, independent living, and economic self-sufficiency.

9. The continued existence of unfair and unnecessary discrimination against the disabled denies opportunities to compete and costs the United States billions of dollars in unnecessary expenses resulting from dependency and nonproductivity.

Purposes of the ADA

There are four purposes of the law based on the aforementioned nine findings:

1. To provide a national mandate to eliminate discrimination against individuals with disabilities
2. To provide an enforceable standard addressing discrimination
3. To ensure that the federal government will play a central role in enforcing these standards
4. To involve congressional authority in order to address the major areas of discrimination faced by people with disabilities.

Definition of Disability

The definition of disability established in the Rehabilitation Act of 1973 is adopted in the ADA. This definition is as follows: Disability means a physical or mental impairment that substantially limits one or more of the major life activities of an individual, a record of such an impairment, or being regarded as having such an impairment.

Under this definition, disabilities include the following kinds of problems: mobility impairments, sensory impairments, mental retardation, and other physical and mental impairments, including hidden disabilities such as cancer, diabetes, epilepsy, heart disease, and mental illness. Individuals who have a history of these disabilities but are no longer disabled, who have been incorrectly classified as having a disability, or who do not have a disability but are treated or perceived by others as having a disability are protected under the ADA.

MAJOR TITLES OF THE ADA

Title One: Discrimination Regarding Employment

No covered entity shall discriminate against a qualified individual because of disability regarding job application procedures, hiring, advancement, discharge, training, compensation, or other terms of an individual's employment. A qualified person with a disability is someone who, with or without reasonable accommodation, can perform the essential functions of a position. Reasonable accommodation involves making existing facilities accessible, providing job restructuring, and offering training materials, equipment, and modified work schedules. Discrimination because of a disability occurs when an employer with fifteen or more employees fails to make reasonable accommodations that would not cause undue hardship.

Title Two: Public Services

No qualified individual with a disability shall, by reason of such disability, be denied the benefits of services, programs, or activities of a public entity. For example, fixed-route transportation systems must purchase buses or rapid rail vehicles that are accessible to individuals with wheelchairs.

Title Three: Private Accommodations and Services

No individual shall be discriminated against on the basis of disability in the full and equal enjoyment of goods, services, privileges, advantages, or accommodations by any person who owns, leases, or operates a place of public accommodation. Public accommodations would be places such as a hotel or other places of lodging; a restaurant, a theater, park, or zoo; and professional offices, schools, food banks, and social services.

Title Four: Telecommunications

Telephones must be available for those with speech or hearing impairments. Special emphasis is placed on telecommunications relay systems that allow for communication between parties, at least one of whom has a speech or hearing impairment.

Title Five: Miscellaneous

This section prohibits retaliation against an individual because of actions related to the Act and charges various parties with preparation of plans, regulations, and technical assistance manuals.

IMPLICATIONS OF THE ADA POLICY

The Americans with Disabilities Act is clearly grounded in the human rights perspective. The ADA, like other civil rights legislation of the past, is aimed at an oppressed group—persons with disabilities—that has been denied equal opportunity to participate in the larger society.

It is significant that under the ADA, persons with disabilities are defined as a minority group. This definition suggests, for example, that if the disabled person is poor, it is less a result of personal inadequacy than of a discriminatory society. Consequently, the adjustment to a disability is not merely a personal problem but one requiring the adjustment of the larger society to the person with disabilities. This position requires that society adjust its attitudes and, as such, remove the obstacles it has placed in the way of self-fulfillment for people with disabilities, including transportation and architecture systems designed only for the able as well as the stereotypes that impugn the competence of people with disabilities (Karger & Stoesz, 1990).

The research suggests that, like other oppressed groups within society, people with disabilities have suffered tremendous discrimination. The National Council on Disabilities the Civil Rights Commission, and national polls all concluded that discrimination against people with disabilities is still pervasive in American society (Pardeck & Chung, 1992). This discrimination is sometimes a result of prejudice or patronizing attitudes, and sometimes it is the result of indifference or thoughtlessness. Whatever the origin, the outcomes are the same: exclusion, segregation, or the denial of equal, effective, and meaningful opportunities to participate in activities and programs. The ADA is aimed at preventing and correcting the numerous problems associated with discrimination against people with disabilities (Pardeck & Chung, 1992).

Another implication of the ADA is the law's focus on the philosophy of empowerment. The ADA is designed to help people with disabilities take charge of their own lives so they can partake of the great bounty this nation has to offer. As recent research (Pardeck & Chung, 1992) has found, "not working" is perhaps the truest definition of what it means to be disabled in America. Ending discrimination against people with disabilities will have the direct impact of reducing the federal government's expenditure of $57

billion annually on disability benefits and programs that are prem-
ised on dependency of the individual with a disability. The ADA
also has the immediate effect of changing people with disabilities
into consumers and taxpayers. Furthermore, "when individuals
move from being recipients of various types of welfare payments
to skilled taxpaying workers, there are obviously many benefits not
only for the individuals but for the whole society" (*Federal Register*,
1980, p. 45). In essence, the Americans with Disabilities Act is aimed
at stopping discrimination against people with disabilities in the
workplace—clearly, an outcome that will help to empower this
group through employment (Pardeck & Chung, 1992).

It is important to note that among the groups protected under
the ADA are people who have AIDS or who are HIV positive. It is
significant that employers cannot discriminate against a person
with these medical conditions.

In the final analysis, the most important implication of the ADA
is that American society is finally changing its views on disabilities.
No longer are people with disabilities seen as individuals who
must be hidden from public view through placement in institutions
or simply as people who should be grateful for the disabilities
programs currently in place. Furthermore, the ADA has the positive impact of correcting the discrimination and segregation that
people with disabilities have endured in the past. The ADA means
that people with disabilities will have the same constitutional
rights and privileges as able people. Just as other minority groups,
such as people of color, people with disabilities have new protections that will help them realize their full constitutional and human
rights (Pardeck & Chung, 1992).

ADVOCACY AND THE AMERICANS WITH DISABILITIES ACT

The goals of advocacy are to achieve social justice and to empower people. Advocacy helps people correct those situations that
are unjust. Achieving social justice through advocacy requires the
active participation of citizens who are vulnerable or disenfran-
chised; the professional social worker also plays a critical role in
this process. The banding together of those who wish to achieve
social justice provides an opportunity for empowerment and for

active, responsible participation in the public realm (Lewis, 1992). The role of the advocate is to speak on behalf of clients and to empower clients to speak on their own behalf when their rights have been denied. The advocacy role is a critical strategy for those who are grounded in the ecological approach to practice because it expands opportunities by protecting the interest of clients. Furthermore, advocacy is a classic role aimed at changing the social environment of clients, including the various ecosystems that prevent individual growth and development.

McGowan (1987) concludes that advocacy can be conducted at two levels: case advocacy and cause advocacy. The case advocacy approach focuses on individual cases. It involves partisan intervention on behalf of a client or identified client group with one or more secondary institutions to secure or enhance needed services, resources, or entitlements. Cause advocacy seeks to redress collective issues through social change efforts and improving social policies.

Rees (1991) argues that case and cause advocacy both begin by identifying the dynamics causing social injustice. Rees makes the following conclusion about the advocacy process:

The decision to pursue the advocacy of a case or a cause, or a combination of both, will usually have been preceded by the identification of an injustice which it is felt cannot be rectified simply by efficient administration or negotiation. The identification of an injustice and the sense of conviction that the removal of this injustice should become a priority, even in a congested workload, goes hand in hand with the advocacy process. It is not sufficient merely to recognize an injustice. You have to believe that this issue should be fought for, and if necessary over a long period of time. (p. 146)

The effective advocacy role involves data collection, effective communication with the public through the media, revenue raising, and building coalitions.

Miley, O'Melia, and DuBois (1995) conclude that the following issues must be an integral part of the advocacy process aimed at social injustice and social change:

1. The location of the problem must be identified. It must be determined, for example, if the problem reflects a personal need, a gap in services, or inequitable social policy.

2. The objectives of intervention must be identified. For instance, objectives might be defined as procuring entitlements for clients or expanding job opportunities for oppressed individuals.

3. The target system of advocacy intervention must be identified. This might be the practitioner's own agency or other systems the agency works with.

4. The advocate must determine what authority or sanction he or she has to intervene in a targeted system. This can include legal rights of clients and judicial decisions.

5. The resources available for advocacy efforts must be identified. These resources include professional expertise, political influence, and one's credibility and reputation.

6. It must be determined by those involved in an advocacy effort the degree to which the target system is receptive to the proposed advocacy effort. The target system will make this decision based on the reasonableness or lawfulness of the advocacy effort.

7. The level at which the intervention will occur must be analyzed to ensure that the desired outcomes will be achieved. Different levels of intervention might include policy changes, modification of administrative procedures, and alterations in the discretionary actions taken by staff or management in an agency.

8. The object of intervention must be identified. This might include individual delivery services, agency administrators, or even a legislative body.

9. The strategies of advocacy intervention must be determined. These strategies include the roles of negotiator, collaborator, and adversary.

10. Those involved in advocacy efforts must learn from the outcomes of prior advocacy efforts, including both failures and successes.

What should be clear from the preceding information is the degree to which the information is consistent with the ecological perspective of social work assessment and intervention. Furthermore, the foregoing points suggest that advocacy is a holistic approach to social change that involves efforts at both the micro- and macrolevels.

Those who are involved in advocacy efforts must understand the need for this type of intervention with the various systems they work with. What must be understood, if one considers the blight of people with disabilities, is that public and private entities did not, for example, ask for the passage of the Americans with Disabilities Act. Most systems located in the public and private sectors, including schools and businesses, would prefer self-regulation over a federal mandate aimed at protecting people with disabilities. Those involved in advocacy find that self-regulation does not work and that even after the passage of legislation such as the Americans with Disabilities Act, social systems mandated to conform to this new disability law will attempt to avoid their legal obligations. This means that advocacy is an absolute necessity to ensure that laws, such as the Americans with Disabilities Act, are implemented appropriately.

There are a number of reasons why entities legally bound by the mandates of civil rights legislation, such as the Americans with Disabilities Act, attempt to avoid compliance. First, organizations (including schools and private businesses) have been provided the compliance materials for the Americans with Disabilities Act; however, they often do not follow compliance materials because such materials may contradict the bureaucratic rules of these systems. For example, the person with a disability brings a unique set of needs to the workplace, including the need at times for special accommodations. Bureaucratic organizations are often rigid systems and are not prone to make exceptions; they literally must be forced to make exceptions through strong advocacy efforts.

Second, all public and private entities bound by the mandates of the Americans with Disabilities Act feel that they operate on limited resources. If an employee with a disability requests a reasonable accommodation in order to do his or her job, the organization understands this to be an added cost. Advocates must play the role of convincing organizations asked to provide special accommodations for people with disabilities that this is a requirement of the law and that the federal mandate for providing special accommodations is based on the needs of the person with a disability and not necessarily the needs of the organization's budget.

Third, people are often intimidated by both public and private bureaucracies. For example, a person with a disability may have limited experience and exposure in dealing with organizations in general. Such persons need the help of an expert—the advocate—in dealing with complex organizations. Skillful advocates understand how complex organizations work and are well aware of the regulations these systems must follow, including disability laws.

Finally, it is often difficult for persons with a disability to look at their own problems without their emotions affecting their objectivity. Skillful advocates are able to step back from situations that negatively affect persons with disabilities and provide reason and objectivity to the process for both the person with a disability and the entity who is not complying with the Americans with Disabilities Act.

Using the Americans with Disabilities Act as an example, the importance of advocacy even after a law has been passed to protect a category of people becomes clear. Advocacy is about influence and power, ingredients that are often critical to forcing entities to conform to regulations and laws.

EXAMPLE OF CASE ADVOCACY

The case advocacy example focuses on a person with a hidden disability who experienced employment discrimination. Under the Americans with Disabilities Act, a disability is defined as a physical or mental impairment that substantially limits one or more of the major life activities of an individual, a record of such an impairment, or being regarded as having an impairment. Hidden disabilities often fall under the second prong of the ADA disability definition: one who has a history of an impairment. The focus of this case advocacy example involves a person who had a history of cancer. This person was denied a promotion to an administrative position. A person who has a history of cancer is fully protected under the Americans with Disabilities Act.

Cancer and Employment Discrimination

What most people do not realize is that for many cancer survivors, job discrimination is often worse than fighting the disease. It is estimated that at least one in four survivors of cancer experiences job discrimination. Some research reports that the numbers of cancer survivors experiencing job discrimination may be as high as 50 percent (Pardeck, 1994).

Job discrimination is common among cancer survivors because of stereotypes and myths. There is one common belief that cancer survivors have high absenteeism from the workplace because of long-term medical problems, but there is no basis for this belief. Many employers and employees have a traditional view of cancer; they simply think that cancer equals death. The general population, including employers and employees, do not realize cancer can be cured or controlled. If given the chance, cancer survivors can lead long and productive work careers. Unfortunately, some employers discriminate against cancer survivors because they simply do not feel comfortable having them in the workplace; there are even some individuals who think that cancer is contagious. Given the myths and stereotypes about cancer, survivors of the disease frequently experience discrimination in the workplace. There are more than eight million cancer survivors in the United states; survivors thus represent a large minority group that has historically experienced job discrimination.

The Organizational Setting

The focus of this advocacy effort was aimed at a large state agency. The organization was highly bureaucratic and generally had a history of lacking sensitivity to diversity and human rights. Specific cases of discrimination were reported on the basis of not only disability but also race and gender. The organization in one case spent over $150,000 defending a charge of racial discrimination and lost. The practitioner suspected that there were other cases of discrimination in the organization that were settled in a discrete fashion unknown to the public. Workers in the agency often described the administrative hierarchy as being stuck in a 1950s mentality toward civil rights. What became clear to the advocate was that the organization had little tolerance for dissent and that the internal due process mechanism for employees was largely a farce.

The model for conducting advocacy intervention is the same model used in Chapter 9, which includes the following:

1. Entering the system
2. Mapping the ecology
3. Assessing the ecology
4. Creating the vision of change
5. Coordinating and communicating

6. Reassessing
7. Evaluating.

Advocacy intervention differs from other types of ecological intervention in that it is not necessarily attempting to treat an individual client and his or her transaction with the larger social environment; rather, it is aimed at achieving social justice and empowering people.

Entering the System

The advocate, during the first stage of the advocacy process, entered the system, a large state bureaucratic agency, and did a detailed analysis focusing on the social relationships within the system. These relationships were the processes that led to the person with a history of cancer being discriminated against in the area of job promotion. As the practitioner assessed these relationships, it became clear that many of the people in authority positions achieved their rank in the organization on the basis of nepotism. This meant that advocacy efforts would be resisted because key administrators had a vested interest in protecting each other even if civil rights law (i.e., the ADA) had been knowingly violated.

An earlier discrimination case in the organization based on race provided insight for the advocate into how the organization would react when challenged in the area of employment discrimination based on disability. The case involving discrimination on the basis of race became public knowledge through the local newspaper. The coverage of the case in the newspaper made it obvious that the administrators in the organization would protect each other at almost any cost. It was also clear that the organization had little understanding of civil rights law. As the news reports concerning the discrimination stated, even after the organization settled the case, which cost over $150,000, the organization did not admit to the discrimination and, more important, made little change in organizational policy to prevent future discrimination.

The dynamics of the case included the following: Specifically, James L., the person with a history of cancer and the focus of the case advocacy, applied for a promotion to an administrative position. The organization was well aware of James L.'s history of cancer. In fact, James L. was asked by a high-ranking administrator if he would be interested in the promotion even before the position was advertised publicly. James L. told the administrator he would be interested; however, he stated to the administrator that he left a prior position of similar rank in another state agency because of the complications related to the cancer recovery process. James L. felt that once this high-ranking administrator found out about his history of cancer, the administrator was no longer interested in promoting him to the administrative position. In fact, a fellow employee in the organization told James L. that a high-ranking administrator had asked if he knew James L. had a history of cancer when the organization had hired him.

The initial strategy was to work within the organization. It was decided that James L. should discuss the discrimination with the human resources officer. The goal of this meeting was to see if the problem of not promoting James L. could be corrected. Another goal was to explore ways that the organization might be more sensitive to issues related to disabilities and to ensure that the Americans with Disabilities Act was being implemented appropriately. After a discussion with the human resources officer, James L. concluded that the organization was not willing to correct its discriminatory acts against him. It also became clear to him that the internal due process mechanism would prove fruitless.

Mapping the Ecology

This stage of the advocacy process involved mapping the ecology, accomplished through systems analysis. In this case, the advocate, through a systems approach, mapped the organization that denied James L. the promotion to an administrative position. During the mapping process, the practitioner placed particular emphasis on the subsystems of the organization.

Important subsystems related to the discrimination were the people involved and the events that took place. To gain information from people involved about the events that took place, the advocate interviewed key informants, including James L. and one of his coworkers.

James L. provided the greatest insight into what had taken place during the job selection process. He stated that he was highly qualified for the position and that he had always received the highest job performance rankings possible within the organization. James L. stated that he was asked by a high-ranking administrator during an informal interview if he was interested in the position, and at the end of the interview with the administrator James L. mentioned his history of cancer. Two weeks after the informal interview with the administrator, James L. officially applied for the promotion to the administrative position. James L. was not even granted an interview for the position during the search process; given this situation, he went to the human resources officer about the dynamics that had taken place during the job selection process. James L. was assured by the human resources officer that his history of cancer had nothing to do with the failure of the organization to grant him an interview or to promote him to the position. As noted previously, James L. felt that the internal due process system designed to resolve job-related complaints within the organization would not work effectively on his behalf.

The advocate also interviewed a key informant who knew the details of how the recruiting process worked. The key informant concurred that James L.'s history of cancer probably played a role in his being denied the promotion. The key informant, however, did add that James L.'s references from his prior job were distorted by influential people within the organization. This distortion allowed those involved in the selection process to justify their actions of not promoting him to the administrative position. Since James L.'s work record within the organization was excellent, the advocate concluded that the distortion of references from his prior job was the organization's strategy to justify its actions of nonpromotion.

Assessing the Ecology

Once the advocate mapped the state agency through a systems analysis, the gathered information was interpreted. The first phase of this process was to analyze the strengths and limitations of the agency. One of the major strengths of the agency was created by the mandates it had to follow from the federal and state governments. Specifically, the agency, under state law, had to have a highly developed personnel policy because it was a state entity. In addition, the agency was mandated to follow federal civil rights law, including the Americans with Disabilities Act. The major weakness of the agency was the use of nepotism for hiring high-ranking administrators. This meant that once the advocate challenged the system, the response by the administrators would be to protect each other because they were indebted to each other on the basis of nepotism. This also meant, from the advocate's view, that the high-ranking administrators would act in a nonrational fashion once challenged. Saul Alinsky (1946), a famous advocate and activist, argued that this is the preferred reaction because it means that those who are challenged by advocacy efforts will make strategic errors.

The advocate also determined that since the administrators in the organization were hired on the basis of nepotism and not merit, their reaction to the advocacy efforts would lack sophistication. The advocate concluded from historical information on prior challenges to the organization based on violations of civil rights law that the agency would spend a great deal of time and resources defending itself even when obvious civil rights violations had occurred. This also meant that many errors would be made by the organization during the advocate's efforts, such as those that had occurred in the racial discrimination case (which cost over $150,000).

Creating the Vision of Change

It was decided that the most productive case advocacy strategy for James L. would be to file a discrimination complaint with the Equal Employment Opportunity Commission (EEOC) under the Americans with Disabilities Act. As noted previously, James L. had discussed his case with the agency's human resources officer and concluded that the agency had no interest in discovering the truth concerning his case. James L. also had little or no faith in the due process procedures the agency used for employees who filed grievances against the agency.

The complaint filed with the EEOC under the Americans with Disabilities Act alleged that James L. was a highly qualified candidate for the administrative position he had applied for within the agency. Not only was he not appointed to the position, but the agency even

denied him an interview. James L. argued that the agency's discriminatory actions were because he had a history of cancer.

Coordinating and Communicating

During this stage of the advocacy process, the major role of the
advocate was to coordinate and communicate with those involved
in James L.'s case. The advocate maintained close contact with
James L. throughout the EEOC's investigation, which took nearly
a year. An important individual the advocate maintained contact
with was the key informant within the agency, who supported
James L.'s claim of discrimination. This key informant provided
valuable information to the EEOC concerning the case.

The advocate also maintained close contact with James L.
throughout the investigation by the EEOC. James L. needed emotional support from the advocate; furthermore, the advocate felt
that retaliation by the organization against James L. was likely to
occur, and it did. This retaliation was in the form of harassment.
Two incidents of harassment occurred, both involving James L.'s
immediate supervisor. The first occurred when James L. was called
into his immediate supervisor's office; the supervisor harassed
James L. about filing the complaint and said he could not understand "why you want to sue the agency." The second act of retaliation occurred when the immediate supervisor announced during
a staff meeting that James L. had filed the complaint; James L. was
present at the meeting, but many who attended the staff meeting
were not aware of the complaint. The advocate determined that
both acts of harassment were retaliation and that additional complaints based on retaliation could be filed with the EEOC. James L.
and the advocate decided that additional complaints would not
help his case, but the information would be used later if the agency
continued harassing him.

Reassessing

After the year-long investigation by the EEOC, the EEOC
granted a right-to-sue letter to James L.; this meant that there was
enough evidence supporting his claim of discrimination that he
had the right to take his case to federal court. At this point in the

advocacy process, the advocate recommended that James L. retain an attorney to help him determine if he wished to sue the agency for discrimination on the basis of disability. James L. had a 3-month time period in which to make this decision.

Evaluating

The final evaluation of James L.'s case was conducted when he had to make a decision about filing a lawsuit in federal court. The advocacy effort was determined to be successful because James L. was granted a right-to-sue letter by the EEOC. Other indirect successes also appeared to result from James L.'s case; specifically, the organization, during the EEOC investigation period of James L.'s case, appeared to place greater emphasis on the importance of fair hiring and promotion procedures. This was evidenced by memos to employees throughout the organization related to employment discrimination and, in particular, by the revisions to the personnel manual. These revisions included new protections for individuals of protected classes in the area of employment, with particular emphasis on protecting people with disabilities from discrimination.

CONCLUSION

Advocacy is a powerful strategy for bringing about social change and social justice. It is an intervention strategy grounded in the ecological approach. Advocacy is aimed at bringing about change in social systems that deny people their basic rights; it is also aimed at expanding the opportunities of the oppressed. Furthermore, advocacy is a powerful role for changing social environments of clients, including the ecosystems that prevent individual growth and development. In other words, advocacy is a critical role for those who wish to use an ecological approach to practice.

As stressed in this chapter, advocacy is a powerful strategy for practitioners to use on behalf of clients whose civil rights have been violated. Even though there are numerous civil rights laws in place, including the Americans with Disabilities Act, public and private entities often attempt to avoid compliance with these laws. Civil rights laws are at times not followed because they contradict bureaucratic rules of organizations, and organizations often perceive these laws as contributing to added costs. When systems fail to comply with civil rights law, the advocate uses his or her influence and the power behind these laws to force compliance. A detailed case example presented in this chapter, using an ecological approach to advocacy, illustrates how the process of advocacy can work on behalf of a person with a disability.

REFERENCES

Alinsky, S. D. (1946). *Reveille for radicals.* Chicago: University of Chicago Press.

Brothwell, D. S., & Sandison, A. T. (1967). *Diseases in antiquity.* Springfield, IL: Charles C. Thomas.

Burgdorf, R. L., & Burgdorf, M. P. (1977). The wicked witch is almost dead: *Buck v. Bell* and the sterilization of handicapped persons. *Temple Law Quarterly, 50,* 995–1054.

Federal Register. (1980). No. 66. Washington, DC: U.S. Government Printing Office.

Fiedler, L. (1978). *Freaks.* New York: Simon & Schuster.

Galdston, I. (Ed.). (1963). *Man's image in medicine and anthropology.* New York: International Universities Press.

Hull, K. (1977). The specter of equality: Reflections on civil rights of physically handicapped persons. *Temple Law Quarterly, 50,* 944–952.

Ianacone, B. P. (1977). Historical overview: From charity to rights. *Temple Law Quarterly, 50,* 953–960.

Karger, H., & Stoesz, D. (1990). *American social welfare policy.* New York: Longman.

Lewis, E. (1992). Social change and citizen action: A philosophical exploration for modern social group work. *Social Work with Groups, 14,* 23–34.

McGowan, B. G. (1987). Advocacy. In A. Minahan (Ed.), *Encyclopedia of social work: Vol. 1* (18th ed., pp. 89–95). Silver Springs, MD: National Association of Social Workers.

Miley, K. K., O'Melia, M., & DuBois, B. (1995). *Generalist social work practice: An empowering approach.* Boston: Allyn & Bacon.

Newman, J. (1987). Background forces in policies for care and treatment of disability. *Marriage and Family Review, 11,* 25–44.

Pardeck, J. T. (1994, July/August). What you need to know about the Americans with Disabilities Act. *Coping,* 16–17.

Pardeck, J. T., & Chung, W. (1992). An analysis of the Americans with Disabilities Act of 1990. *Journal of Health and Social Policy, 4,* 47–56.

Rees, S. (1991). *Achieving power: Practice and policy in social welfare.* North Sydney, Australia: Allen & Unwin.

Sussman, M. B. (1965). *Sociology and rehabilitation.* Washington, DC: American Sociological Association.

Index

About the Author

JOHN T. PARDECK is Professor of Social Work in the School of Social Work, Southwest Missouri State University. He is the author or co-author of numerous books including *Issues in Social Work* (Auburn House, 1994) and *Computerization of Human Services Agencies* (Auburn House, 1991).

ISBN 0-86569-236-X

EAN

HARDCOVER BAR CODE